THE

ULTIMATE BLUEPRINT

Insanely FOR AN

SUCCESSFUL

BUSINESS

KEITH J. CUNNINGHAM

Great Operators
Get Tired

Great Business Owners
Get Rich!

KEYS TO THE VAULT.

Published in the United States by Keys to the Vault Publishing
www.keystothevault.com
Keys to the Vault is a registered trademark of KJC Investments, Inc.

Submit all requests for reprinting to:
Keys to the Vault Publishing
P.O. Box 30527
Austin, Texas 78755

Cover design by Sheila Parr

Publisher's Cataloging-In-Publication Data

Cunningham, Keith J.
   The ultimate blueprint for an insanely successful business /
Keith J. Cunningham. — Second edition.

pages : illustrations ; cm

"Great operators get tired. Great business owners get rich!"
Issued also as an ebook.
ISBN: 978-0-9846592-5-8 (Hardcover)

1. Success in business. 2. Business enterprises—Finance.

3. Accounting. I. Title.

HF5386 .C86 2014
650.1   2014945576

Printed in the United States of America on acid-free paper

14 15 16 17 18 19   10 9 8 7 6 5 4

Second Edition

For Sandi . . . IWLYF!

Contents

Introduction

"My Business Is Running Me!"

"I don't feel like I'm running my business. I feel like my business is running me. I'm whipped!"

If you're in business, you have, on more than a few occasions, gritted your teeth, hung your head in exasperation, and mumbled those three sentences.

Over the past forty years, I have had the opportunity to advise, counsel, and teach thousands of business owners across a wide range of industries, from technology and retail to wholesale and distribution. And through it all, I hear the same thing from business owners everywhere: They're tired and they're frustrated! They feel like they own a job and not a business. Whether they're breaking even in San Diego or making millions in Sydney, whether they're just getting started or have been in business for decades, the complaint is the same.

Not one of these owners suffers from a lack of passion about their idea or a lack of operating expertise. They work hard . . . really hard! Most business owners are great operators. That's why they decided to go into business in the first place. They're great at what they do and they love doing it. 🔑 But the problem with being a great operator is that you don't get rich, you get tired.

Great business owners get rich. They are successful in business because they know how to run the **business** end of their business. They understand and use the critical business skills and tools required to create sustainable financial success. Sure, anyone can get lucky. But even the lucky ones eventually must find a way to sustain that good fortune before their luck runs out.

Here is the key: 🔑 Sustainability always comes from *knowing* what you are doing and *measuring* your progress. Businesses don't run themselves, and tragically, most business owners don't know how to run them either. So they bounce around, lurching from one new marketing strategy or bright idea to the next, and eventually the business fails because the owner quits or dies from exhaustion.

I also meet a lot of entrepreneurs whose primary focus is on getting rich. That's a shortsighted goal. 🔑 The goal of owning a business isn't just to be successful, it's to be successful and *stay* that way. I have no interest in being successful for a week (or healthy for three days or in a great relationship for a month). I want what I want for the rest of my life.

If you're good enough at what you do, if you understand the business end of your business, if you throw in a little luck, and if, if, if . . . you might get rich. As Charlie Munger says, "Business is highly complex, and anyone who says it's easy is stupid." Staying good at anything requires learning the *right* skills and then practicing them over and over. If you want to succeed at ping-pong, you've got to learn and practice ping-pong skills. If you want to succeed at chess, you've got to master and practice chess skills. No matter how many hours you spend perfecting your forehand slam, it's never going to make you a grandmaster at chess.

Business is no different. For a business owner, the right *business* skills and tools are mandatory. So is practice. And, as with all activities, including business, we must be able to know if what we are practicing is helping us get better or making things worse.

It turns out the key to all this learning, practicing, and sustainability revolves around the ability to *measure*. ⚷ If you want to sustainably succeed in business, you must learn how to measure your financial results, identify the activities that are sabotaging them, and then know how to correct those mistakes so that the results you desire can be achieved. Ultimately, how much you have to spend has very little to do with what you make and everything to do with what you keep.

It all comes down to measuring. Never forget this:

⚷ Measure Results, Change Activities

As a business owner, you might get an accounting report card every month (or at least you *should* be getting this report card monthly, preferably by the tenth of the month). Unfortunately, business owners are notorious for their inability to understand their accounting report cards. They spend tens of thousands of dollars each year on accounting and bookkeeping, and all they get is a tax return. What a waste!

☞ Your financial results are simply a numerical reflection of the business decisions and operating activities in your business.

Consider this sequence:

Management makes decisions. Decisions get converted into activities. Accountants and bookkeepers then record these activities on your accounting report card as financial results. Accounting is the process of converting business activities into numbers and reporting them on the accounting report cards. ☞ Financial and business analysis is the process of converting the numbers on the accounting report cards back into activities. The *purpose* of measuring is to know what to change!

In other words: Good Activities = Good Numbers. Bad Activities = Bad Numbers. I'll be more blunt: Good Management = Good Numbers. Bad Management = Bad Numbers.

☛ My experience is that business failure is more often a result of a bad business owner than a result of a bad business. Don't believe me? Take a look at your industry and count the number of businesses that are knocking the cover off the ball. Sure, there are some differences between your product and theirs. They are in a different location than you and might have more money in their bank account. You are better in some areas, and they are probably better in others. But the primary difference between you and your competition is *you* and your *management team.*

So, let me ask, is your business the reason you are tired, frustrated, and struggling? Or is it you? I heard a sage quip, "The reason most self-employed business owners are unhappy is because they have a lousy boss." I am a huge fan of Paul "Bear" Bryant, one of the greatest college football coaches who ever lived. He famously said, "On any given Saturday, I'll take my team and beat your team. Or, I'll take your team and beat my team." Now that was a man who understood what I'm talking about. The horse rarely causes success; the jockey wins the races.

This is crucial to understand. ☛ Ultimately, management drives the results of any business, and management cannot change those *results* without first changing the *activities* that caused them. Guessing and second-guessing about the problems is a sucker's game and will not produce the results you want. The role of measurement is to provide you with the optics so you can see what to change.

☞ Business is an intellectual sport; anyone who plays this game with their emotions, gut, and glands gets killed. There is simply not a way to get lucky sustainably. Someone once told me that "gut" is an acronym for "Gave Up Thinking." I agree.

☞ Acquiring the skills and tools to understand and measure your financial results is the key to knowing which activities need to change in order to produce superior profits and sustainable cash flow. The numbers don't lie!

Ignorance is not bliss. ☞ Facts don't cease to exist just because you ignore them. Certain things, if you don't know them, can cost you dearly. But if you do know them, they can create a serious competitive advantage.

Business owners and management teams simply do not have the luxury of a blindfolded "Pin the Tail on the Donkey" decision-making strategy for running the business end of their business. The environment is changing too quickly, margins are too tight, and the competition is too fierce to rely on a haphazard "maybe I'll get lucky" approach to business success.

We have all had this experience: You don't know something—whether it's a game or how to operate a machine—and you struggle to make the thing work. Then you learn one little distinction or skill and everything changes. Little things do not mean little results. One strategy, skill, or distinction in how you do something can change the whole game.

Those strategies, skills, and distinctions are the subject of this book. What this book will do for you is what a blood test, MRI, X-ray, and CT scan do for a medical doctor. ☞ Knowing what to measure, what it means, and what to do about it allows you to look beyond the obvious to find the hidden, but deadly, problems that are silently sabotaging your business's financial results.

The Ultimate Blueprint for an Insanely Successful Business will guide you to the answers to these questions:

- How can I be smarter and more competitive?

- How can I add more value and make fewer mistakes?

- How can I rapidly find the leaks that are costing me profits and cash flow? How can I get them permanently plugged?

- How can I take the guesswork out of my decision making and take control of my business and finances?

- What are the critical drivers I must monitor to optimize and maximize my profits and cash flow?

- How can I be more efficient with my business prioritization and activities?

- How can I move the needle with the least amount of wasted motion?

Learning and executing the skills I will teach you in *The Ultimate Blueprint for an Insanely Successful Business* is like going to the doctor for a physical. Knowing how to locate and correct the *systemic* problems (which cause you to feel lousy and run down and, if left untreated, can kill you) is critical to long-term business success. In contrast, concentrating on sales and marketing is analogous to going to a fitness gym. It's not that being buff isn't important; it is. ⚷ It's that a maniacal obsession with growing sales and revenue does not treat the primary causes of the insanely high business mortality rates nor ensure the business's health, sustainability, and longevity.

So why should you listen to me? Because I have made the same mistakes you're making, and I had to figure out a way to create sustainable financial success without killing myself or destroying my businesses. I've started, owned, financed, turned around, sold, and purchased scores of businesses over the past forty years. I have made some good business decisions and netted a fortune, and I also made some bad decisions and lost it all.

In the 1980s, I was investing in real estate and made millions. Then, two things happened. Number one: I got greedy. Number two: I started ignoring the risks. I began to think I was bulletproof. I knew the party wasn't going to last forever; I just thought I was smart enough to dodge the hangover. I forgot to look at what could go wrong and became obsessed with what could go right. As Bill Gates says, "Success is a lousy teacher. It lulls smart people into thinking they know what they're doing." I'll say it differently: 🔑 Success only teaches bad lessons. I found out the hard way that emotions and a knack for innovative financing, mixed with unbridled greed, produce economic disaster.

That was twenty-five years ago. I regrouped, licked my wounds, learned my lessons, and rebuilt. I attribute 100 percent of my subsequent business and financial success to mastering and practicing the critical business skills, tools, and distinctions I am writing about in this book.

I am a business owner. I do what I teach. I divide my time between running the businesses we own and Keys to the Vault®, which is our business school for business owners. I teach and advise business owners how to significantly improve the results of their business by acquiring the critical *business* skills and tools necessary to produce sustainable success. I do not "operate" any of our businesses. (Operators get tired!) I run the business end of our businesses. You should check out our Keys to the Vault® website, www.KeystotheVault.com, (or Chapter 18) for the curriculum of the business courses I teach. They are game changing!

There are a lot of books on the market and "experts" on the speaking circuit who claim to share the "secrets of success" or "how to get rich in fifteen minutes a week without ever breaking a sweat." I understand there is even such a thing as a "4-hour work week," which is a great idea if your competition is only knocking out two. I'm here to tell you that stuff is nonsense. 🔑 Business doesn't have a magic formula or a secret recipe. There's no financial tooth fairy. Succeeding in business is highly complex. Anyone who tells you otherwise wants to sell you something.

So why isn't there a secret formula for business? Well, unlike sports, where the boundaries of the field or width of the goal posts never change, the environment for business is always shifting. A good idea a year ago could be a bad idea today. 🔑 The only constant in business is change, which is why business is an *intellectual* sport.

There are, however, fundamentals, principles, and rules that if you learn, practice, and master, will significantly improve your odds of creating a sustainable business and financial success. When you know better, you do better.

Throughout this book, I will highlight these key fundamentals and principles for you with this symbol: 🔑.

At the end of the day, you'd like your business to be successful for decades. That's the ultimate goal for all of us. My goal is to take the complex issues of running the business end of your business and turn them into plain English. *The Ultimate Blueprint* will teach you how to produce Harvard MBA results without all the accounting and Harvard MBA mumbo jumbo. Your success is dependent on understanding and implementing the critical business and financial analysis tools, skills, and strategies used by the pros.

If you read this book, you will learn these tools, be able to pinpoint the unique financial problems in your business, diagnose the cause, set the strategy, correct the activities, and radically improve your profits and cash flow—without having to increase revenue.

Learn what I am teaching in this book and you will eliminate the guesswork so you know exactly what needs to be done and the how, when, and why to improve your profits, cash flow, and financial performance. If you understand the accounting report cards you receive every month from your accountant or bookkeeper, you will dramatically close the gap on understanding which activities to correct to produce superior and sustainable financial results.

The Ultimate Blueprint will support you in acquiring the business optics required to make better decisions and thus make more money. And, at the conclusion of this book, I will introduce you to CFO Scoreboard®, a tool that will radically improve your ability to understand and measure your financial results with a minimum amount of brain damage.

⚷ If you master the information in *The Ultimate Blueprint,* your chances of business and financial success increase dramatically. If you don't master it, your chances of frustration and failure are almost guaranteed.

Chapter 1

Creating Leverage

The only difference between a small business and a large business is leverage. That's it. The product, service, or industry could be similar, the machinery or building could be the same, and the logo could be identical. ⚷ What distinguishes a large business from a small business is simply that the large business is able to utilize leverage while the small business doesn't.

Leverage is simply any tool, technique, or process that allows you to do more with less. One form of leverage is other people, or "OP." The most famous example used in business is "OPM" or "Other People's Money." The reality is that there are many other forms of "Other People" leverage, such as other people's time, other people's networks, other people's resources, other people's customers, or other people's brains.

Systems are another form of leverage. Unfortunately, some people make the mistake of *over*-systemizing their business. Systems are notorious for draining flexibility and passion from a company.

Think of the employees at McDonald's, and you'll see what I mean. McDonald's is the most systematized business in the world and it's the one-trick pony the systems freaks trot out to justify their "systems are the holy grail" concept. If you only need your employees' arms and legs, systematize away. But if you need their heads and their hearts, be gentle in how aggressive you are with systems. Used in moderation, they can be a great form of leverage.

After my "do-over" in the 1980s, I started a *Log of Lessons Learned*. I decided a foundational key to my ultimate success was to avoid repeating my prior mistakes. I wanted twenty years of experience, not one year's experience repeated twenty times!

One of my earliest and most important lessons was this: ⚷ What costs me money is what I don't see.

Today I have that as a screensaver, so that I notice it every time I look at my computer. A bright red marquee scrolls across my screen asking *What Don't I See?* The biggest "What Don't I See?" is my assumptions, so I continuously ask myself the following question: What assumptions am I making that I'm not *aware* I'm making?

My assumptions have cost me money: my assumptions on what is broken or what could go wrong, my assumptions on what is producing the success I have or what could disrupt that success, my assumptions on what the fix is or my ability to execute that fix. To minimize the "What Don't I See?" and the faulty assumptions, I have come to rely on two things:

⚷ Measuring Time and Thinking Time are the two highest forms of business leverage available.

So, you sit at your desk long after everyone else has gone home for the day, and you stare at a stack of bills. Or maybe you're making good money with your business, but the cash flow is inconsistent and lumpy, with two good months followed by a horrible one. Or, you have your sights set on a certain financial goal, and even though you have made progress, you're not getting there fast enough. You're working your butt off, you're a selling machine, but things aren't improving. One month after the next, the problems remain the same.

The answer to the above is always measuring time and thinking time.

I'm a big fan of measuring. Of course, you can overdo measuring, too. You can take it to its illogical extreme and start measuring too much or too frequently or even measuring things that aren't meaningful. ⚷ But knowing *what*, *how*, and *when* to measure is one of the highest forms of leverage, because that is the only way to know whether or not what you're doing is producing the desired results and moving you in the desired direction. ⚷ Measuring is the primary key to sustainability. You can't sustain something unless you know what's working and what isn't, and the only way to know for sure is to:

1. Measure your progress and results.

2. Identify, correct, and improve the activities that are causing those results.

3. Measure your progress and results.

4. Identify, correct, and improve the activities that are causing those results.

5. Measure your . . . you get the idea.

Thinking time is the other primary leverage tool you should add to your business tool belt. 🗝 My experience is that getting and staying rich is a result of avoiding doing stupid things, and stupid mistakes are a result of faulty assumptions—things that seemed like good ideas at the time. So, here it is on a bumper sticker: All my problems started out as good ideas. How about yours?

Don't believe me? I'll ask you the same question I've asked thousands of people in my courses, speeches, and presentations around the world: How much money would you have right now if you hadn't squandered it on bad investments and ill-conceived, "looking good," impulsive, instant gratification expenditures (all good ideas at the time)?

🗝 Our problem is not that we don't have enough opportunities to make money. Our problem is that we have too many opportunities to lose it. In fact, one of the biggest problems with being rich is that the number of ways you have to lose money expands exponentially. It's easier than you imagine to self-sabotage your wealth, especially if you're ignorant about your assumptions.

Warren Buffett has two rules: Rule #1: Don't Lose Money. Rule #2: See Rule #1. I'm going to add Rule #3: **THINK!**

As I've said, business is an intellectual sport. Napoleon Hill's beloved book, still a bestseller after more than seventy years, is titled *Think and Grow Rich*. It isn't "Use Your Gut and Grow Rich," or "Sit in a Dark Room, Om, and Visualize a Sack Full of Money Dropping on Your Head and Grow Rich," or "Do What You Love and Grow Rich." It's *Think and Grow Rich*!

Too many people make the mistake of believing they can somehow get rich and stay rich by ignoring the facts, doing what comes naturally, or simply doing what they love. Business doesn't work that way. The advice of "do what you love and the money will follow" is questionable, at best. That is analogous to saying "eat what you love and be skinny" or "sleep with whomever you want and have a great marriage." Not exactly sound advice for creating success, but man, will it sell books! Doing what you love might make you feel fulfilled. It might make a great hobby or pastime. You might feel energized and excited. You might make a huge contribution, but simply loving to *do* something will not create financial success.

🔑 Thinking time allows me to sidestep problems before they arise, or to identify the root cause of problems, if I haven't already dodged them. Measuring is the tool that allows me to face reality and correct the activities that are causing my problems.

My experience is that businesses that create and sustain success have an owner and management team who:

- 🔑 Look for problems and crises *before* they arise and act or correct accordingly. Thinking time requires being skeptical about what might go right and seriously considering what might go wrong. It is a lot less painful (and expensive) to avoid a problem than it is to correct it.

- 🔑 Face reality by consistently measuring the current result.

The trick is to understand and know how to find the underlying cause that produced the offensive outcomes and then change the appropriate activities to produce better results in the future. Some people hate to measure, so here it is on a bumper sticker: ⚷ Anyone who doesn't want to measure doesn't want to be held accountable.

Leverage takes many forms, but the two most powerful for any business owner are thinking and measuring. Both take time. Both require practice to master, but the results are stunning. Schedule some thinking time on your calendar this week. Question your assumptions. Think about the *real* problem. Set aside some time to start candidly facing the reality of your business by measuring your results and reverse engineering those results to find the activities that need to change.

Now, let me make the case for measuring, since that is the primary topic of this book.

Chapter 2

What Gets Measured Is What Gets Done

Ninety percent of all businesses fail within ten years of start-up. That's nine out of ten businesses! The statistics are alarming. Yet every business owner thinks they're invincible. It's like not wearing a seat belt and rationalizing, "Someone else might get in a wreck, but it's not going to happen to me!" Business owners use the same faulty logic regarding business mortality rates. "Ninety percent may fail, but it won't happen to me!" Quick, name five businesses in your town that are more than fifty years old. It's very hard to do, which proves my point. Businesses go out of business at an alarming rate.

It *can* happen to you. Here's why. The only constant in business is change. The business environment, competition, consumer preferences, key suppliers, interest rates—they're all constantly changing and the speed of change is accelerating. **⊶** Sustainability is impossible without measurement.

Charles Darwin's manifesto on the theory of evolution is about "survival of the fittest." However, the fittest does not mean the strongest, biggest, smartest, or richest; it means the most adaptable and the most flexible. Flexibility and adaptability—in nature or in business—require paying close attention to the environment, knowing exactly where you are, being acutely aware of what is and what isn't working, and changing whatever is necessary to survive and thrive. ⚷ If you do what you have always done, you will fail.

The primary way for you to know how to adapt to change is to measure your results so you know where you are and what is and isn't working. But you also have to know which activities to change to produce better results. Simply measuring your results is not enough.

That's why anyone who is a master at what they do is a measurement freak. Peyton Manning. Oprah Winfrey. Warren Buffett. They're always measuring, comparing and tweaking. If you read Buffett's annual report to shareholders, you'll see the whole thing is filled with measurements and comparisons: How he's doing today versus how he did last year. This quarter versus the same quarter a year ago. Month over month. Current performance versus projected performance. Buffett understands that the slightest numerical variation can mean the difference between stupendous success and catastrophic failure.

The same thing is true for *your* business. Without measuring, how will you know if you're getting better or worse and, equally important, what caused these changes and what should you do about them?

At its most basic, ⚷ business optics relies on measuring the trends and relationships between the numbers . . . knowing *what* to measure, *how* to measure, *what it all means,* and *what to change* so that the appropriate problem is identified and the offending activity is corrected. In a nutshell, 🔑 measure the effect and change the cause. It's that simple.

🔑 What gets measured is what gets done. What gets measured is what gets managed. Most people are not getting the right things done or prioritizing what gets managed, which explains why they are tired, struggling, and frazzled. They are running their business like an operator instead of a business owner. They don't know what to do next because they're not measuring their results.

If you step on the scale and weigh 5 pounds more than you did last week, you've got a choice. Either keep eating the Krispy Kreme donuts and gain another 5 pounds or give up the donuts. The solution is obvious, right?

To us it is. But that's only because we know the cause-and-effect relationship that allows us to adjust our nutritional activities to change our weight results. If you don't know anything about nutrition or dieting, you won't be able to draw a direct line from those Krispy Kremes to your weight gain. You may decide to wear different color socks or start watching television with your shirt turned inside out in an attempt to burn off those extra calories. "Maybe this will work!" you think, blindly lurching from one scheme to another, hoping that you'll get on the scale and discover that those 5 pounds have magically disappeared. You don't know *what* to change to get different results.

If you persevere long enough, you might eventually stumble onto the right combination, but it's going to take forever. And that's exactly the kind of haphazard, random action that wears out business owners. They are simply guessing and second-guessing, which is exceptionally time-consuming, mind numbingly frustrating, and ultimately useless. They're stressed and exhausted because they don't know how to locate and prioritize the activities (causes) that will then produce the desired results (effects).

If you knew what to measure, you'd find the process infinitely faster and more efficient. **⚷** Measuring allows you to see exactly where you are, if you are getting better or worse, what needs to be corrected, and what it's costing you not to change. It enables you to say, "Here's where I want to move the needle, and here are the activities I need to adjust to accomplish this outcome." That's business optics, and that's what this book is about.

⚷ To create the results you desire

1. Get clear on where you are—measure.

2. Decide where you want to go—your goal.

3. Identify the root problem that is blocking this progress—the cause.

4. Tackle the problem—execute.

5. Determine your progress—measure.

That's it.

So where do you start? **⚷** When it comes to business and financial optics, everything starts with the numbers. If you can't understand the numbers, you can't speak the language.

Chapter 3

If You Can't Read the Scoreboard, You Don't Know the Score

Business is a game. As in any game, there are winners and losers. There is fierce competition and a set of rules. There are bad moves, good moves, and better moves. Strategy is critical. Execution is paramount. And, of course, there are scoreboards.

Name one competitive sport in which you play the game hoping to win, where you never glance at the scoreboard, or if you do, you don't have a clue what it says. Can you imagine a Super Bowl where the scoreboard stops functioning moments before kickoff, and the announcer says, "Don't worry about it; no one looks at it anyway"?

And yet, that's how most people play the game of business. No wonder 90 percent of all businesses fail and the vast majority of the balance struggle to survive.

Imagine going to your doctor because you've been feeling dizzy and light-headed. She runs some tests, gives you a quick once-over, and says, "Actually, I'm not sure how to interpret these test results. But you know what? You look okay to me. I'll see you next year." You'd fire the doctor for incompetence.

Sadly, this is exactly what most business owners do. They get the numbers from their accountant, and then they have no idea what the numbers mean. It's like the hapless doctor who casually eyeballs a patient to diagnose his health problems. A good doctor is adept at reading and understanding the test results and, based on that interpretation, diagnosing the cause of the problem and prescribing a remedial activity. Is his cholesterol 600? Start exercising, lose 10 pounds, and take Crestor. Is his blood pressure 175/120? Cut down on the salt, start exercising, lose 10 pounds, and take Mavik. None of these diagnoses are available without doing the blood tests. But blood tests are useless if you don't know how to interpret the data. If you don't know how to analyze the results or if you have no benchmarks or standards to which you can compare them, what good are they?

Most business owners are frustrated because they see the *results*, but they don't have a clue about the activities that *caused* them, so they don't know what to change. They have no idea how much money they're leaving on the table as a result of not correcting an underlying problem. They cannot prescribe the right medicine until they accurately diagnose the disease.

Accurate financial analysis is key to the health of your business. It's about looking beyond the obvious and knowing, "If I tweak this, I can double my profits. If I adjust that, I can triple my cash flow." You can only get those sorts of clear, simple solutions with business optics and financial analysis—not only by looking at the numbers but also by knowing what they mean.

Tragically, too many business owners have subscribed to the bathrobe theory of business—one size fits all—which says that whenever there is a problem, "Grow!" Conventional wisdom seems to dictate that growth is the answer, regardless of the question. The "Kool-Aid" that the growth experts recommend for superior financial performance is to tweak the website, change the advertising copy, tweet and blog more frequently, hire a new graphic artist to redo the logo and brochure, rejigger the sales commission structure, add two new salespeople, and grow revenue at all costs. ⚷ Having only a throttle in your business cockpit and assuming that doubling the amount of horsepower in your engine will cause your business to go twice as fast is seductive but delusional.

Attempting to create business success by *solely* relying on the growth lever is a little like trying to become Mr. Universe by entering a hot dog-eating contest. You may get bigger, but it's highly unlikely you're going to win the title you want. So why do so many business owners and entrepreneurs obsess about size and speed? There are three primary reasons:

1. They are stuck in adolescence. Sales and traction are critical in a business start-up phase, but maturity requires a balanced approach. Take football. Everyone starts learning the game by throwing and catching (and fantasizing about the glory of scoring the winning touchdown). As teams and players progress, the vast majority who win championship titles have developed

tremendous depth, balance, and defense. Think of revenue and sales as the offense and business optics and measuring as the defense. You need both to win.

2. It feeds the ego. Who doesn't imagine, "Look how important and famous I will be when I'm big." In business, size does matter, but the yardstick includes profits and cash flow, not just revenue.

3. It's fun. Making a baby is always more exciting than raising one. Changing the diapers and 2 a.m. feedings don't get the headlines, but they are the reality of parenting. Whacking expenses, eliminating waste, avoiding unproductive assets, collecting accounts receivable, building and refining corporate culture, and listening to customer complaints are the reality of business.

As fun, exciting, and important as sales and marketing are, gorging yourself on growth rarely solves financial problems. I see a lot of businesses struggle and fail, not because they aren't adding new customers but because the owners are lousy at keeping the ones they've got. Don't believe me? 🔑 How big would your business be if you still had every customer who ever tried you? I rest my case.

The goal is not to get big. The goal is to create sustainable success. And you can become really, really successful being really, really small. And you can go really, really broke becoming really, really big.

An old mentor of mine used to tell the story of a company that made less and less on more and more until they finally went broke getting rich. It happens more often than you'd think. Look no further than General Motors for a prime example of a business that forgot that the point of being in business was to make money, not get big.

Here is my critical point: 🔑 Big ≠ Success.

The great business owner has a cockpit full of dials and levers. He or she knows there are a number of things to test and measure; it's not just about going full speed ahead. Growing your business in the absence of clear optics is an accident waiting to happen, whereas if you become efficient and optimize your results and *then* grow your business, you just might grow rich. As Warren Buffet says, "I would rather own a $10 million a year business making 15 percent than a $20 million a year making 5 percent." That's what I call playing to win.

Remember I said that business is a game? In addition to scoreboards, strategies, rules, and competition, there is a language. In fact, all activities have a language. Cooks understand mincing, dicing, quarts, and teaspoons. Astrophysicists understand quarks, black holes, and neutrons. Concert pianists understand the bass and treble clef, sharps and flats, and a little Italian for good measure. The world's most successful people are fluent in the language of their respective fields.

Business also has a language. If you haven't already guessed it, 🔑 the language of business is accounting. If you can't speak the language, you can't play the game.

But here's a warning: If the key to getting rich was only learning how to speak the language, then all accountants would be rich. And they're not. So it isn't.

The trick is to learn how to translate that language into something that's usable. It's an accountant's job to convert activities into numbers and then put those numbers on the three financial "report cards"—the balance sheet, the income statement, and the cash flow statement. Those report cards, however, don't tell you which answers you got right, which ones you got wrong, or what to do to get a better grade. You've got data but no optics.

Trouble ensues because business owners don't speak the language. Therefore, they don't know how to reverse engineer the financial statements they receive from their bookkeepers and accountants and thereby see the underlying problems in the business.

Every number on your accounting report card is a result of some activity. There are no alien numbers, no UFOs that fly onto a balance sheet. ⚷ If you're not happy with the numbers you're getting, the question has to be this: What activities need to change in order to produce better results? There is no way to win this game by guessing.

⚷ *"If you can't read the scoreboard, you don't know the score. If you don't know the score, you can't tell the winners from the losers."*

—Warren Buffett

⚷ If you want to permanently close the gap between where you are and where you want your business to be, it's mandatory that you start paying attention to the scoreboard of your business.

Chapter 4

The Language of Business

Have you ever listened to two accountants talk to each other? It's an exercise in futility. You might as well be listening to people from a remote Scottish village. You know they're speaking English, but you don't have a clue what they're saying.

The following scenario might sound familiar. You get your accounting report cards from your accountant or bookkeeper at the end of the month—your income statement, balance sheet, and (maybe) cash flow statement. You look over the paperwork and see some numbers you don't like and don't understand. So you call up your bookkeeper or accountant and say, "Hey, how did this happen?"

Your accountant says, "Great question. I'll tell you exactly how that happened. We debited this and credited that. Then we did an adjusting journal entry and posted the whole thing to the trial balance, and 'poof' there you go." Highly accurate but not exactly helpful.

To answer your questions, your accountant is likely to attempt to explain it to you using the only words they know. And if you don't understand what those words mean, you're in trouble. *Debit* and *Credit*. For such small words, debit and credit are extraordinarily confusing. To make it simpler, I like to use the words "increase" or "decrease" instead. Forget about whether or not you will debit or credit something. Instead ask, "Is the number in this particular account or category going up or is it going down?"

Bottom line—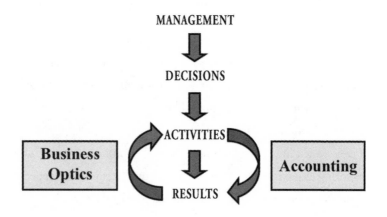 accountants take transactions and financial activities and turn them into numbers and then place those numbers on the financial statements. That's what you're paying them to do.

MANAGEMENT

DECISIONS

ACTIVITIES

Business Optics

Accounting

RESULTS

The purpose of business optics (which is *not* the role of most business accountants but is *your* job as the business owner) is to take those numbers and turn them back into activities. If you don't know what the activities were that caused the numbers in the first place, you have no shot at correcting the problem.

Knowing that your cholesterol is 600 is meaningless unless

a. You know what it means.

b. You have a benchmark to compare it to.

c. You know what caused it.

d. You know what to do to change or control it.

0—π The real solution lies in knowing which direction the things are headed, where they should be, and what activities need to change in order to move the numbers in the right direction.

The same logic applies to any of the numbers on your accounting report cards. Receivables of $10,100. Profits of $15,116. Assets of $69,500. Cash of $44,655. Without a frame of reference, what do these numbers mean? Are they good or bad? Compared to what? Are they better or worse than they used to be? How do I change them and make my business more successful?

I am making a very important point here: **0—π** Ultimately business optics come down to two things:

- comparing the trends over time

- measuring the relationships between numbers within a time period

THE BALANCE SHEET

So let's take a moment to understand the report cards prepared by the accountants. First, look at your "balance sheet."

On the left-hand side are "things and stuff."* The things and stuff of your business are Cash (you can spend it), Accounts Receivable (money owed to you by your customers), and Inventory (stuff you

---

*I first came across the concept of "Things and Stuff" from Marshall Thurber.

BALANCE SHEET	
THINGS AND STUFF	**OWE**
Cash	Accounts Payable
Accounts Receivable	Taxes Payable
Inventory	Notes Payable
Property/Plant/Equipment	**OWN**
	Owner Investment
	Earnings—Current
	Earnings—Retained

have bought that you intend to resell). Then there are the physical things and stuff like Property, Plant, and Equipment. Every business has some things and stuff.

Now the question is this: Do you "owe" or do you "own" your things and stuff? Look at the right-hand side of the balance sheet.

You might owe money to your vendors and suppliers (Accounts Payable). You might owe money to the government (Taxes Payable), or you could owe money to a lender or a bank (Notes Payable).

If you don't *owe* on your things and stuff, then you must *own* it. In accounting, a business owns three things:

1. The investment made by the shareholders, investors, or owners;

2. The earnings (or profits) the business has earned in the current time period (for example, month, quarter, or year); and

3. The earnings from all prior time periods, that have been retained in the business.

So the left-hand side of a balance sheet is comprised of things and stuff, and the right-hand side is what you owe and own. In the language of accountants, your things and stuff are called "assets," what you owe are "liabilities," and what you own is "equity." (In some countries, equity is known as "net assets.")

The left-hand side of a balance sheet always equals the right-hand side . . . it balances!

In other words, *things and stuff* always equals what you *owe* <u>plus</u> what you *own*. Or said another way, *things and stuff* <u>minus</u> what you *owe* equals what you *own*.

THE INCOME STATEMENT

A second accounting report card is called an "income statement."

INCOME STATEMENT
Revenue (Sales)
−   Expenses
=
Profits
Net Income
Earnings
Bottom Line

Here is where it can get tricky. Sometimes accountants call this report card an "income statement" and other times they call it a "profit and loss statement," a "P&L," or a "statement of operations." These are all the same thing.

An income statement records the revenue (or sales) activities of a business along with the expenses (or costs) incurred to produce that revenue. For this report card to be meaningful, the revenue produced is "matched" to the costs and expenses incurred *during a specific time period.* Measuring doesn't work too well if you're trying to figure out what you ate sixteen years ago that caused you to be 5 pounds overweight today.

The same is true for the income statement. We're looking for the specific costs that occurred in connection with specific sales during a specific time period (typically months, quarters, or years), and we want to have them grouped onto the same income statement report card.

If the revenues exceed the costs, then there is a profit (or earnings or net income). If costs exceed revenue, then there is a loss. Either way, whether it's a profit or a loss, it's commonly referred to as the "bottom line."

THE CASH FLOW STATEMENT

The third accounting report card in the arsenal of an accountant is called a "cash flow statement."

CASH FLOW STATEMENT	
Beginning Cash	x
Operating Cash Flow	+ / −
Investing Cash Flow	+ / −
Financing Cash Flow	+ / −
Ending Cash	y

Cash can come from different sources and be used for different things. You will notice in the previous diagram, there are three broad categories of cash flow.

1. The first is "operating cash," which can be generated from sales or by collecting accounts receivable, and can be used for paying expenses or accounts payable. (These examples are not intended to be an exhaustive list but rather illustrative to help you understand the concept.)

2. The second type of cash flow is "investing cash," which can be generated by selling certain assets and can be used to buy certain assets, like a vehicle, real estate, or a piece of machinery.

3. And finally there is "financing cash," which can be generated by borrowing money from the bank or by raising money from an investor and can be used to repay money to the bank or distribute money to an investor.

🔑 Since the cash flow statement is like a movie (versus a snapshot) of what happened to the cash of a business, it will cover a certain period of time, such as a month, quarter, or year. If we start the time period with some beginning cash and then add or subtract the amounts of operating cash flow, investing cash flow, and financing cash flow either generated or used *during* this time period, we will wind up with the ending cash at the end of the time period. We will cover cash more thoroughly in later chapters but here's something to ponder in the meantime: Not all cash is created equal!

⊙━ An income statement is also a movie (not a snapshot). It covers the exact same time period as the cash flow statement. An income statement is the movie of the total revenues and expenses *during* a particular time period (typically a month, quarter, or year).

⊙━ A balance sheet, however, is not a movie. It's a snapshot. A balance sheet records the assets, liabilities, and equity of a business *as of* a specific moment in time. A balance sheet might say "as of December 31, 2013," or "as of April 30, 2013."

At the start of the two movies (the income statement and cash flow statement), there is a snapshot of the *beginning* balance sheet. At the end, there is another snapshot called the *ending* balance sheet.

A complete set of accounting statements for the calendar year 2013 would look like this:

Beginning Balance Sheet as of 1/1/13	Income Statement for 1/1/13 to 12/31/13	Cash Flow Statement for 1/1/13 to 12/31/13	Ending Balance Sheet as of 12/31/13

The beginning and ending balance sheets serve as brackets or bookends for the income statement movie and cash flow statement movie.

Now that you're familiar with the three report cards, how do they all fit together?

On a balance sheet in the lower right-hand corner in the *own* or equity section is the word "earnings." There are actually two types of earnings and they are shown as two separate lines in the equity section of a balance sheet:

1. Earnings in Current Period—the earnings or profits that happened in the current time period covered by the current income statement, and

2. Retained Earnings—the earnings or profits that have accumulated and been retained by the business in all the previous time periods.

You will notice that the income statement calculates the earnings of a business in the current time period. It turns out that the number on the ending balance sheet for "earnings in the current period" is the exact same number as what was reported on the income statement as the "bottom line." It looks like this:

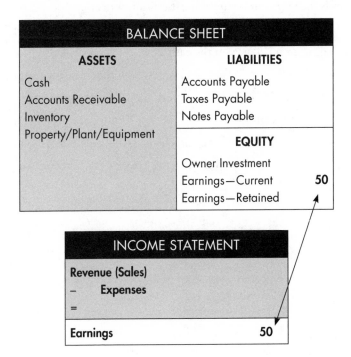

So we might say that the current earnings displayed on a balance sheet are a world atlas of the earnings in the current time period and the income statement is the street map of those earnings. In other words, the balance sheet might show that your earnings in the current time period are 50. The income statement would tell you exactly how much you had in revenue and all the costs and expenses incurred during this time period to produce and service 50 in earnings.

You will also notice that the balance sheet has a category in the upper left-hand corner under "Assets" called "cash." As we just discussed, one of the movies that accountants prepare is called a cash flow statement.

It turns out that the ending cash number on the cash flow statement is the exact same number as the amount of cash reported on the ending balance sheet. If the cash on the ending balance sheet is 75, the ending cash balance on the cash flow statement will also be 75.

The cash flow statement shows you how much cash you started with at the beginning of the period and the amount of cash you added or used during the current period from operating, investing, and financing activities. If we add the beginning cash balance to the cash we generated or used during the current time period, we will then see the ending cash balance on the cash flow statement. Once again, the balance sheet serves as a world atlas and the cash flow statement is like a street map. It looks like this:

BALANCE SHEET	
ASSETS	**LIABILITIES**
Cash 75	Accounts Payable
Accounts Receivable	Taxes Payable
Inventory	Notes Payable
Property/Plant/Equipment	**EQUITY**
	Owner Investment
	Earnings—Current
	Earnings—Retained

CASH FLOW STATEMENT	
Beginning Cash	x
Operating Cash Flow	+ / −
Investing Cash Flow	+ / −
Financing Cash Flow	+ / −
Ending Cash	75

So if we connected all three accounting report cards together, we would see this:

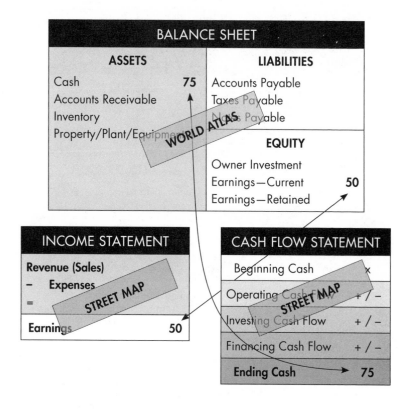

If you stop to think about this, ⊶ all financial transactions of a business impact the balance sheet in some way. If the transaction has something to do with revenue and expenses, it will also impact the income statement. If the transaction has something to do with cash, it will also impact the cash flow statement.

The balance sheet has a category to record the amount of cash a business has. The balance sheet also has a separate category to record the amount of earnings a business produces. Furthermore, accountants have one report card to keep track of profits or earnings and a different one to keep track of cash. The monetary amounts in these two categories and the monetary amounts in these two report cards are not the same number. The obvious conclusion is

🔑 Earnings are not the same as cash.

As we will discuss in Chapter 6, you cannot spend your profits; you can only spend cash. As you are about to find out, 🔑 your profits are the *theory* of whether your revenue did or did not exceed your expenses. 🔑 Cash on the other hand is a *fact*. Making this distinction between profits and cash will fundamentally shift your perspective and allow you to start thinking about and managing the business end of your business in an entirely new way.

Suppose we wanted to have a complete set of financial statements for the first quarter of 2013 (Jan–Mar). At a bare minimum, here are the requisite accounting report cards we would need to get started:

Beginning Balance Sheet as of Jan. 1 2013	Income Statement for the 3 months of Jan. 1 2013– Mar. 31 2013	Statement of Cash Flow for the 3 months of Jan. 1 2013– Mar. 31 2013	Ending Balance Sheet as of Mar. 31 2013
Snapshot	Movie	Movie	Snapshot
"As of…"	"For the 3 months of"	"For the 3 months of"	"As of…"
World atlas	Street map	Street map	World atlas
	Theory	Fact	

But, as we will see in Chapter 5, the bare minimum is not enough. It doesn't do any good to get the numbers and then not know:

- what the numbers mean.

- what needs to be measured.

- how to measure.

- which numbers are important.

- how to change the important numbers.

- which levers to pull to improve your results.

Accounting systems like QuickBooks, Xero, and MYOB are financial transaction *recording* tools, not financial or business *optics* scoreboards. Once you have a basic understanding of the accounting report cards and what they do, it will be a lot easier to figure out how to implement a system that measures your results and alerts you to specific activities you can change so that you can produce better financial results.

🗝 If you cannot measure your results, you will either continue to struggle or you will fail because key information goes undetected.

Let me be clear about one more thing: Understanding the basics of accounting report cards will not make you rich. On the other hand, being ignorant about financial and business optics and analysis will definitely impede your ability to maximize or sustain any wealth you do create.

🗝 Understanding the measurements, identifying the real problems, and knowing precisely which levers to pull and dials to turn is critical to radically accelerating your profits and cash flow.

When you have finished reading this book, you will have ten to fifteen game-changing strategies you can successfully implement on your own. *Immediately!* You are to about to learn one of these strategies in the next chapter on the power of trends.

Chapter 5

The Trend Is Your Friend

Have you ever put together a jigsaw puzzle? The first thing you do after you dump out all the pieces is to get them all "right side up" so you can see the colors and patterns. Your next step will probably be to find the four corners and straight edges. Then you start organizing the pieces by color or patterns to match the picture on the box. Your strategy is to arrange the pieces in such a way that you can solve the puzzle with the least amount of brain damage.

To solve the business optics puzzle, let's begin with some basics. Namely, how your financial information is laid out and presented to you.

Take a look at the most recent income statement you received from your accountant or bookkeeper. There's one column of numbers, right? Revenue, cost of goods sold, gross profit, rent, payroll, marketing expenses, employee benefits, website hosting, and so on. And finally, profits.

You have an income statement. So what?

A column of numbers does no good whatsoever if you don't have a point of comparison. With no frame of reference, you don't know what it means that your profits were $176 or that your revenue was $147,613.

Think about the last time you made a significant purchase, like a house or a car. Before you made your decision, you shopped around and looked at a number of different houses and cars, right? You didn't walk into the first house you saw with a "For Sale" sign and say, "Yep! This is it, I'll take it." In order to make an informed decision, you had to compare and contrast. Same thing with a car. You don't buy one until you've done a number of test drives. It's why people looking to begin a relationship go on numerous dates. They're comparing and contrasting potential partners.

Most business owners, however, do not receive their financial information in a format that allows them to compare and contrast. They typically get one column of numbers—the current month, quarter, or year. A few of you *might* get a second column of numbers—year-to-date results. This is woefully inadequate.

🔑 Business optics and financial intelligence start with multiple points of comparison over numerous time periods.

To be meaningful, these comparisons must be on a single piece of paper or spreadsheet. Comparing this month's income statement to last month's is a pretty good comparison. But an even better comparison would be to compare this month's income statement with last month's and the month before. And even better than that would be to compare this month to last month to each of the *six* months before that.

If you have eight, ten, or twelve columns of numbers instead of just one, you now have multiple points of comparison and the ability to spot trends. On the income statements for the businesses we own, I use up to 18 columns or time periods. I have a column for each of the past five years of annual historical income statements and a column for each month of the current year plus an additional column on the far right-hand side of my spreadsheets for the year-to-date total. So, if it's June 2014, I've got the income statement numbers for 2009, 2010, 2011, 2012, 2013 and for January, February, March, April, May, and Year-to-Date Total 2014 displayed on a single page. I have multiple points of comparison so I can easily see how I *am currently* doing in comparison to how I *previously* did. That's the only way to know whether I'm getting better or worse. And if my income statement is detailed enough about various expenses, I can start zeroing in on where specific issues and problems are hiding.

⚿ Without multiple points of comparison, I have no optics, rendering my financial statements useless. Your balance sheet, income statement, and cash flow statement all must display multiple time periods, side by side, to be meaningful. **⚿** Trend analysis is the first component of business intelligence. The *trend* is your *friend*.

⚿ The second key to business optics and financial intelligence is to display your income statement in four different formats:

1. The first format shows the total "dollar" amounts (in the currency you use—dollars, yen, euros) for multiple time periods.

2. The second presentation averages your results so you can easily compare the four or five previous years (or quarters) with the monthly results in the current year.

3. The third presentation should be in percentages, and the best way to do this is with a technique called "common size." Common sizing your income statement means converting every monetary amount to a percentage of total revenue. If revenue is $1,000,000 and cost of goods sold (COGS) is $750,000, your COGS is 75 percent of revenue. If rent is $25,000, then rent would represent 2.5 percent of revenue. Knowing that a particular expense has gone up or down by a specific monetary amount is useful, but seeing the expense represented as a percentage of revenue is critical to seeing the magnitude of each expense in relation to revenue.

   ⚷ Common sizing is the second most powerful income statement financial analysis tool available to you to drive profitability.

4. The fourth presentation of an income statement should be in "dollars per unit." Let's say you're in the restaurant business. If your "per-unit" measure is number of customers, divide every line item or account on the income statement (for all revenue and all expenses) by the number of customers served in the time period.

   ⚷ Dollars-per-unit analysis is the single most powerful income statement analysis tool you have to control and drive profitability, bar none.

If you can see your revenues and expenses on a per-unit basis, your brain can now go to work on strategies and adjustments that will knock pennies per unit off your labor costs, for example, or add pennies per unit to your revenue. A few cents per unit one way or the other is a significant number to your bottom line. Knowing you're spending $31.37 in labor on a per-unit basis is exponentially more powerful than simply seeing a lump number of $23,952 on an income statement.

Walmart has perfected the art of per-unit revenue/cost analysis. Like any successful organization that has demonstrated sustainable success, Walmart measures. When they're stocking their stores, they ask questions like, "If we increase the square footage of the Coca-Cola display by two inches, and we take two inches away from Pepsi, are we going in the right direction on the sales per square foot?" It really is that specific; they know exactly how many dollars per square foot Pampers is generating in revenue, and exactly how many dollars per square foot Huggies is providing. And they know what happens if Crest toothpaste is moved up or down on the shelves or closer to the endcap or more toward the middle of the aisle. Performing some R&D (I'm referring to research and duplication here) on what the big boys are doing is a good idea, and all the big boys are measuring on a per-unit basis.

🔑 Measuring revenue and expenses per unit over an extended period of time is a game-changing idea that will spark your ideas and put profits in your jeans.

I know what you're thinking: "Keith, this is a lot of work." It's true, and that's just one more reason why I created CFO Scoreboard®.

We display your financial information in a trend format and do the "common size" and "per-unit" calculations for you. CFO Scoreboard® will also display the monetary changes from one time period to the next and identify which specific expense, revenue item, or balance sheet account needs immediate attention. CFO Scoreboard® is about one thing: providing you with better decision-making optics so you can make better decisions and more money.

⚿ Trend analysis allows you to figure out where you're getting better, where you're getting worse, and how much money you're leaving on the table as a result of not fixing the problems. Organize all your income statements into one spreadsheet. Set up all your balance sheets onto a second spreadsheet. Put all your cash flow statements onto a third spreadsheet. And make sure you have all three. Most business owners don't receive all three accounting report cards, and if they do, they never look at them. ⚿ Don't fall into the trap of thinking that what you don't see can't kill you. It can, and it will—and it hurts.

Once you've gathered the right information and consolidated it in one central place, your odds of having the optics to successfully solve this puzzle increase dramatically. It all starts with getting the information organized and presented so you can see the trends. Now let's take a look at building *The Ultimate Blueprint for an Insanely Successful Business*.

Chapter 6

The Ultimate Blueprint for an Insanely Successful Business

When business owners receive their accounting report cards (probably inconsistently) and when they bother to peek at them (even rarer), they glance at the income statement and the first place they look is the lower right-hand corner. The bottom line. Net income. Earnings. Profits. If it's a good number, they have a drink. If it's a bad number, they have two drinks. The thinking (and drinking) seems to be predicated on the idea that the profit a business produces is the most important number on their accounting report cards. This is dead wrong and helps explain why so many businesses struggle.

The net income of a business is simply the result of some math. Why in the world would I get excited or depressed about the number 4? Maybe the revenues were 1,000 and expenses were 996.

Another business's revenues might be 15 and the expenses 11. They both have the exact same net income of 4. While the profit number is important, what is critical is how we got there.

🔑 Profits are a result of how *efficiently* management is controlling the expenses on a given amount of revenue. Revenues are a result of how *effectively* management is utilizing the business's assets.

🔑 There is one primary reason for a business to have assets: to produce and service revenues. Why else would you have your things and stuff? Certainly there might be times when your assets are acquired to produce a cost savings, and when this is the case, your assets' function is to ultimately increase profits. But, by and large, your assets are for revenue (sales) production.

Some businesses are "service" (versus bricks-and-mortar or manufacturing), and therefore have very few physical assets on the balance sheet in the things and stuff section. For these kinds of service businesses (and for most others as well), the single most important asset we have is our people or employees. If you stop to think about it, the primary role of our employees is also to produce revenues or to service the revenues we receive, and thereby, help us to produce more profits.

🔑 So, the purpose of assets is to produce revenue and the purpose of revenue is to produce profits.

🔑 *The Ultimate Blueprint for an Insanely Successful Business* is to acquire (or employ) assets that are highly *effective* at producing revenue and then *efficiently* convert those revenues into profits.

There's just one problem with this formula: You can't spend your profits. You can only spend cash. Just because your profits have a "dollar" sign in front of them does not mean they are cash. Profits have nothing to do with cash.

⚷ Profits are a theory, cash is a fact.

Profits are the theory of whether or not the revenues in your business exceed the expenses. If they do, then you have a positive profit, net income, or bottom line. If they don't, you have a loss. Your business probably has some accounts receivable (which is money owed to you by your customers who gave you an IOU instead of cash). These IOUs should have been recorded as revenue on your income statement at the time of the sale even though you didn't receive the cash. (This assumes you are using "accrual accounting." In Chapter 11, I'll explain why this is the *only* method of accounting you should be using.)

And it is just as likely that you charged some expenses to a credit card or gave one of your vendors an IOU. This is called an account payable. These expenses were still costs, even though you didn't use your cash. In other words, an income statement is designed to tell you the *theory* of your revenues, expenses, and profits. It is not designed to tell you whether or not these profits have been converted into fact (cash). That's the job of the cash flow statement.

IBM's income statement is a theory. Google's income statement is a theory. Microsoft's income statement is a theory. And your company's income statement is a theory too.

So here is *The Ultimate Blueprint for an Insanely Successful Business:*

ASSETS

REVENUE

PROFITS

CASH FLOW

It looks simple, but what it really means is that you need to be very *effective* at acquiring assets that maximize and service revenue, then be very *efficient* at converting those revenues into profits, and finally be very *productive* at converting profits into cash flow.

As business owners, we're ultimately trying to convert our assets into cash flow. That's *The Ultimate Blueprint.*

🔑 But the key distinction is this: Not all cash is created equal.

The mistake that most small business owners make is failing to differentiate between the different kinds of cash.

As I said in Chapter 4, there are three kinds of cash: operating, investing, and financing. In other words, there are three different places cash can be generated or used in a business. For example (and these examples are not exhaustive), operating cash is generated by revenue or used to pay expenses. Investing cash is generated by selling your property, plant, and equipment assets, or used when buying more of these kinds of assets. And financing cash has to do with borrowing from or repaying banks, or raising funds from or distributing money to investors.

Of the three cash categories, operating cash is the mother lode. **⊶** Operating cash flow measures a business's ability to convert profits into cash.

In fact, a good business is a business whose operating cash flow is not only positive but also bigger than its profits. A bad business, on the other hand, always struggles to produce positive operating cash flow. Or worse—it has negative operating cash flow. Without positive operating cash flow, you're either:

1. Delaying paying your bills.

2. Dipping into savings to pay your bills.

3. Selling some of your things and stuff to pay your bills.

4. Borrowing money from the banks, friends, or family to pay your bills.

5. Raising money from investors to pay your bills.

⊶ When you are out of cash, you are out of business. That's the definition of bankruptcy. There's no cash to pay your bills and no ability to borrow more money to pay off the money you have already borrowed. No business can survive and sustain itself in the long term without successfully converting its profits into operating cash flow. Yet, the vast majority of business owners never realize there are different kinds of cash or understand the importance of converting profits into *operating* cash flow. They're just buying another round at the bar, because they glanced at the bottom line on the income statement, saw a positive number, and decided to celebrate. Dumb!

Think about the following scenario: Is it possible for a business to have $50,000 in profits and have no cash? Sure it is. Maybe a big customer you thought was going to pay you hasn't yet. Or maybe you bought too much inventory, so even though you've got $50,000 in profits on your income statement, all your cash was spent on next quarter's inventory. Maybe you purchased a new vehicle for $75,000 and used all your cash for that.

Here's the corollary: Could you have $100,000 of losses and $200,000 of cash? Absolutely! You might have just borrowed $200,000 from the bank, or maybe you didn't pay a large bill you owed one of your vendors. Having profits move in the opposite direction from cash happens all the time.

🔑 The bottom line is that cash and profits have absolutely nothing whatsoever to do with each other.

When it comes to the blueprint for your business, you have to pay close attention to not only the size of each number but also the *growth rates*. You don't want—on a percentage basis—assets to grow faster than your revenues. If this happens, your assets are becoming less and less *effective*. You don't want your revenues—on a percentage basis—to grow faster than your profits. When this happens, your revenues are becoming less and less *efficient*. And you don't want your profits—on a percentage basis—to grow faster than your operating cash flow. If this is the case, your profits are becoming less and less *productive*. Obviously there could be short periods of time where one of the above scenarios occurs, but in the long term, any of the above trends are deadly.

⚷ In a well-run business, you want to cascade your *percentage growth rates* so that operating cash flow is growing faster than profits, profits are growing faster than revenues, and revenues are growing faster than assets (regardless of whether those assets are buildings, machinery, people, or payroll dollars).

As an example, we'd like to have our assets (or number of employees or payroll dollars) remain constant, but have our revenues grow by 10 percent, our profits grow by 20 percent, and our operating cash flow grow by 30 percent. That's a well-run business. A poorly run business would be where assets (or number of employees or payroll dollars) grow by 50 percent, revenues grow by 10 percent, and profits only grow by 2 percent, leaving operating cash flow to stagnate or, even worse, decrease.

⚷ As business owners, we want to have as few assets as possible (regardless of how "assets" is defined) producing the maximum amount of revenue. If I have $1,000 of assets and I'm selling gourmet coffee beans, I'd like the assets to produce $5,000 of revenue. If I can produce $6,000 or $10,000 of revenue on that same $1,000 of assets, even better. If I could produce $10,000 of revenue with only $500 of assets, I don't need $1,000 of assets and I probably spent too much on my assets. I want the greatest amount of revenue for the assets that I have, and this is true regardless of whether or not I'm talking about physical assets or employee assets. Where business owners get into trouble is when they buy a $4,000 piece of equipment when the $1,000 model would have been more than sufficient. We'll talk more about that in the next chapter.

⚷ At the end of the day, we want to minimize the monetary amount of assets required to produce the maximum amount of revenue. Once we have revenue, we want to minimize our expenses to maximize our profits. Finally, we want to maximize the cash that our profits produce.

The equation looks like this:

Assets **Effective** > Revenue **Efficient** > Profits **Productive** > Operating Cash

This sequence is *The Ultimate Blueprint for an Insanely Successful Business*. It's our job as owners and management to be on a never-ending quest to become more *effective*, more *efficient*, and more *productive*. How do we do that?

You can start by avoiding what I call the "pimp factor."

⚷ Overspending on assets and expenses sabotages your business and financial success.

Chapter 7

The Pimp Factor

We all know the story. A new business owner needs a computer in order to launch her consulting business from home. So she jumps online, goes to BestBuy.com, and sees an $800 laptop that will do everything she needs it to do. But then her eyes start to wander, and before long she notices a $4,000 computer with all the bells and whistles—more RAM, a 17-inch LED display, Bluetooth, fingerprint sensor, backlit keyboard, shiny chrome finish. It's everything she's always dreamed of in a computer. She whips out her credit card and buys it on the spot.

Strike one. She's just sabotaged her business.

Business owners are seduced by the pimp factor. It happens when they pimp their business like rockstars pimp their ride. They get the pimped-out laptop instead of the basic one that does the job. They choose the art deco, ergonomically correct, custom-made designer chairs for their waiting room instead of shopping at IKEA. They need a vehicle to make deliveries, but instead of buying a used van for $10,000, they spend $45,000 on a new one with tricked-out wheels, leather seats, and a state-of-the-art sound system.

The instant you make this mistake, you're setting yourself up for failure. 🔑 You cannot create a sustainable business or optimize your financial performance by overspending on your assets.

Given a choice between a business with $1,000,000 of assets and a business with $10 of assets, which one would you rather have? Don't be too quick to answer. It all depends on the amount of revenue produced and, ultimately, the size of the profits generated by those revenues.

	Business A	Business B
Assets	$1,000,000	$10
Revenue	$500,000	$500,000
Profits	$100,000	$100,000

To make this easier to grasp, assume you had to write the check to acquire these assets to produce these revenues and profits. If Business A has $1,000,000 in assets that will produce $500,000 of revenues and $100,000 of profits, and Business B requires only $10 in assets to produce $500,000 of revenues and $100,000 of profits, I'll take the $10 deal every day. Your banker, on the other hand, would love for you to have Business A so they could justify loaning you money against these assets. I don't happen to be in business to make my lenders rich. And if you find a $10 asset with this kind of revenues and profits, please give me a call!

🔑 My point is that business success is not about the stuff you have. While it's fine to have nice things, you have to be careful that your ego doesn't get overly invested in what you buy and how good you look.

🗝 Too much money makes you stupid. I've seen it time and time again. Look at what happened in the late 1990s during the dot-com bubble. The Internet whiz kids were flush with investor money. But instead of buying a used card table and folding chairs, they went out and bought rooms full of conference room chairs for $1,000 a pop. Instead of being resourceful, they threw money at their problems. And where did those no-hit wonders go? Straight into the dirt, but they sure looked flashy doing it, didn't they?

The reason most business owners pimp their office, car, or computer is because they let their emotions and ego dictate their expenditures. What's the harm, right? Wrong. Strike two. 🗝 The problem with ego-driven expenditures is that they reduce flexibility.

🗝 Think of every dollar you spend as money you're *investing* in your business and all investments produce a *return*. Ask yourself, is that $1,000 ergonomic chair going to produce more revenue? Does it help you reduce your costs or drive profits? Is it going to produce a greater return on investment than a folding chair and a card table? I doubt it.

I know hundreds of business owners who, upon learning from their accountant that they have an unexpectedly large tax bill, will race out and purchase a brand new pickup truck to get the "tax write-off." But the new truck costs $40,000, and the taxes saved are $10,000. Are you kidding me? This makes as much sense as making mortgage payments of $50,000 a year on your house, so you can "get the deduction" and save $12,500 a year on your tax bill. Why would you want to spend $1 of cash to get back $.25? That's a bad investment!

Warren Buffett, the greatest business and investing mind of our time, has it figured out. Buffett's company, Berkshire Hathaway, has an estimated value of $200 billion and employs over 260,000 people. In his annual report for 2010, Buffett revealed to shareholders that his total expenditures on office equipment at the home office in Omaha over the previous forty-five years were $301,363. That's not what he spends each year. That's the *total* that Buffett invested in furniture, computers, printers, artwork, you name it, over *forty-five years*. I know business owners whose companies are only worth $2 million, and they've spent more than Buffett in the past six months on artwork and personal vehicles alone.

Warren Buffett believes that every dollar he spends on fancy chairs is one less dollar he can invest in his business. Smart man.

⚷ Once you've spent it, you can't take it back.

If you spend $500 on the hottest new iPhone package, that's $500 you no longer have to invest in your business. And you can't get a refund on that investment. I'm not anti-Apple or anti-iAnything. But you can't suddenly decide that a $40 Nokia would make and receive calls just fine and then go back to the iPhone store and get your money back. Overspending on assets is like smoking cigarettes: You can't return all the cigarettes you've smoked. But you *can* stop smoking and get healthier lungs.

⚷ In order for us to achieve the success we want, one of the first things we have to do is leave our ego and the need to impress others at the door.

⚷ You have a choice: You can create lifestyle, or you can create wealth. At some point you can have both (if that's what you want), but at the *creation* stage, the two are mutually exclusive. Most people try to straddle the fence—spending on their lifestyle while simultaneously attempting to create wealth. That's like going on a diet and cutting back to only half a dozen Krispy Kremes every day. Those who have become truly successful created their wealth first and then grew their lifestyles. They have understood that money is never spent, it is only invested. And investments either produce a return or they don't.

 Successful business owners invest in things and stuff that enhance the revenue, the bottom line, and the cash flow of their business.

Fancy offices, hot cars, lots of staff, and high overhead are not the definition of success. Spending money to *look like* a big deal is not the same as *being* a big deal. Conserve cash, especially during the good times. As a very smart man once told me, "How you run your business during the good times is a great indicator of how well you will survive the bad times."

Without exception, every big business starts small. Every single one. The average Fortune 100 business began with less than $25,000 of capital. But a primary differentiator is that the Fortune 100 companies invested their money in things and stuff that would magnify and grow their revenues, profits, and cash flow, not their egos. The businesses that ignored this fundamental law did so at their own peril. And they folded long before they ever had a shot at playing with the big boys.

 You have a choice: Look good or get rich.

Choose wrong, and it's strike three, you're out. You lose the right to mutter and complain that your business is struggling and you're not rich. Watch your cash closely. 🔑 For every purchase, ask yourself, "Do I really need this? Will this help me make more money?" Because once you spend it, the cash is gone.

Chapter 8

Building the Scoreboard

As I've said, business is a game; it follows, then, that every company has a score. The score tells business owners how they're doing. Are they winning or losing? Are they leaving money on the table? Are they operating at peak performance? In what ways could the financial results of the business be improved? The place to start measuring your score is with *The Ultimate Blueprint for an Insanely Successful Business* sequence I showed you in Chapter 6.

ASSETS

⬇

REVENUE

⬇

PROFITS

⬇

CASH FLOW

When I ask business owners about their company's financial scoreboard, most don't have a clue what I mean, or if they think they do, they whip out their latest income statement. Accounting financial statements are *not* scoreboards. They are report cards. They just report test results. As with all report cards, accounting report cards don't tell you what questions you missed, what the right answer is, or where the problems are.

When I evaluate a business, the first questions I ask are:

- 🔑 How *effective* is management at acquiring assets and converting those assets into revenues?

- 🔑 How *efficient* is management at converting those revenues into profits?

- 🔑 How *productive* is management at converting profits into cash?

Then I look for the trend for each over the past several months, quarters, and years.

Let's take these one by one. Here's the formula we use to measure *effectiveness*:

🔑 Revenues ÷ Assets = Effectiveness %

You want your assets to be as *effective* as possible at producing revenue. Ideally, you would like to increase your revenues from $100,000 to $130,000 without increasing assets. Or, you would like to increase your assets by 10 percent and receive a 30 percent bump in revenues. (Remember, assets might be stuff on a balance sheet, number of employees, or they could even be payroll dollars spent.)

Obviously you want this *effectiveness* percentage to be as high as possible, and you want this ratio to be trending up month over month and year to year. Pimping your assets destroys this formula and ultimately your business.

Next, when we look at how *efficient* management is at converting revenues into profits, what we're really asking is this question: How good are you at controlling your expenses? Here's the formula we use to measure efficiency:

⚷ Profits ÷ Revenues = Efficiency %

Obviously you want your *efficiency* percentage to be as high as possible, and you want it increasing month over month and year over year. If you're like most business owners, however, your primary strategy to increase this efficiency ratio is to ramp up sales and ignore expenses. Dumb!

As a business owner, you're constantly trying to make the assets you have more *effective* at producing revenues and the revenues you have more *efficient* at producing profits. When both work in tandem, you dramatically increase the odds of creating a sustainable and profitable business. Now, what if we multiplied how *effective* you are times how *efficient* you are? That is the third ratio I calculate to determine a business's score. Here's the formula:

⚷ Effectiveness × Efficiency = Return on Assets

or

$$\text{⚷} \quad \frac{\text{Revenue}}{\text{Assets}} \times \frac{\text{Profits}}{\text{Revenue}} = \frac{\text{Profits}}{\text{Assets}} = \textbf{Return on Assets}$$

If you can remember back to your high school algebra, you know that the two "revenue" amounts cancel each other out and what you're left with is Profits ÷ Assets. Profits divided by Assets is the definition of Return on Assets. When the financial community refers to Return on Assets, they are basically measuring how *effectively* and how *efficiently* the business's assets are being deployed to generate profits.

But as you already suspect from *The Ultimate Blueprint,* this isn't the entire story. Profits are a theory and cannot be spent. So your ultimate goal is to convert your profits (or earnings) into operating cash flow. Here's the formula we use to measure *productivity*:

⚷ Operating Cash Flow ÷ Profits = **Productivity %**

Obviously you want this *productivity* percentage to be as high as possible, and you want it to be increasing month over month and year over year.

A great scoreboard for your business will enhance your optics and laser-focus management's attention. ⚷ The foundation for building a great scoreboard is thinking about and measuring all three ratios: *Effectiveness, Efficiency,* and *Productivity*. With this scoreboard you significantly increase the odds of creating a sustainable, profitable, and cash-flow-positive business.

There's one more way to measure a business: What if we multiplied how *effective* you are times how *efficient* you are times how *productive* you are? Here's the formula for that:

$$⚷ \text{ Effectiveness} \times \text{Efficiency} \times \text{Productivity} = \frac{\textbf{Operating Cash Flow}}{\textbf{Assets}}$$

Or, using the entire formula:

$$\text{�} \quad \frac{\text{Revenue}}{\text{Assets}} \times \frac{\text{Profits}}{\text{Revenue}} \times \frac{\text{Operating Cash Flow}}{\text{Profits}} = \frac{\textbf{Operating Cash Flow}}{\textbf{Assets}}$$

� Your job as a business owner is to maximize the operating cash flow your business generates and minimize the amount of assets it takes to do it. To the extent your assets creep up, you will damage your returns and impair this ratio. To the extent your expenses are mismanaged or ignored, your profits will diminish or disappear and undermine your financial viability. To the extent your operating cash flow is compromised by accounts receivable, inventory, or accounts payable, you will have no cash to pay your bills and that, too, will erode the ratio and compromise your sustainability.

As you already know from Chapter 5, the trend is your friend, and no number has meaning unless you have a comparative reference point. The scoreboard you are building is no different. You must have the ability to compare how your current financial results relate to prior periods' results.

� Ultimately, a great business scoreboard will give you optics and clarity on the following questions:

1. What is the effectiveness, efficiency, and productivity of my business?

2. How does the effectiveness, efficiency, and productivity of my business compare with multiple prior time periods?

3. Is there a way to increase my revenues without increasing assets, employees, or payroll, or can we reduce the amount of assets and maintain the same amount of revenue?

4. Are my assets and revenues effectively and efficiently producing the maximum amount of profits?

5. Is there a way to increase my profitability by decreasing expenses?

6. Are my assets, revenues, and profits productively producing the maximum amount of operating cash flow?

7. Are each of these relationships improving and getting stronger?

8. How can I increase these ratios?

Answering these questions requires doing the *measuring*, identifying the problems, and then *thinking* about the solutions.

🔑 To win this game and actually drive the financial success your business is capable of achieving, cash flow—on a percentage basis—must grow faster than profits; profits—on a percentage basis—must grow faster than revenues; and revenues—on a percentage basis—must grow faster than assets.

🔑 So you might say that a business has three bottom lines, not one. Staring at the profit figure on your most recent income statement is a waste of time. As we've seen above, your real bottom lines are found by measuring the *trend lines* of the following:

1. *Effectiveness* of your assets (Revenue ÷ Assets)

2. *Efficiency* of your revenues (Profits ÷ Revenue)

3. *Productivity* of your profits (Operating Cash Flow ÷ Profits)

If the *trends* you're seeing on your scoreboard are inferior scores, if your results are eroding from where you used to be, you must dig into the numbers and find the activities that need to change so that you can correct the problems and produce better scores. What's caused that dip in effectiveness? Why has your efficiency fallen off the cliff? How can you have profits but be struggling to meet payroll?

What's changed? Is it the environment? Consumer demand? Market competition? Your suppliers? Sure, all of those things are possible. But it could also be that you are doing something differently that has caused the loss of those percentage points. And these are the points that are costing you the game.

🔑 My favorite questions to ask business owners after I have studied their financial scoreboards and spotted a downward trend are these: If you did it before, why can't you do it again? What could you begin doing differently to regain those lost percentage points?

🔑 Build the scoreboard. Measure the results. Change the activities.

Experts at building financial analysis scoreboards will tell you there are numerous additional calculations available that will help you drill into your accounting report cards.

They are right. CFO Scoreboard® will *automatically* give you these optics as well.

Chapter 9

Maximizing Profits

Imagine you had a choice of two vehicles to get you where you needed to go: a tricycle or an F-16 fighter jet. At first glance, we're all attracted to the F-16 because it's a lot flashier, the trip would be exciting, and we would get from here to there much faster. But let's think about this before we fire up the engines.

It takes no expertise or training to ride a tricycle. Anyone can do it. There's no cockpit. Just about the only thing you need to know how to operate is the little thumb bell mounted on the handlebars. A tricycle doesn't go very fast, and operating one doesn't require a huge amount of practice or sophistication. The good news is that if there's an accident on a tricycle, the worst that can happen is a bunged-up knee.

Compare that to an F-16. A fighter jet goes very fast, and if there's an accident, someone is going to die. That's why the pilots who fly F-16s receive extensive training and log thousands of hours practicing in a simulator. They're working with a heck of a cockpit—hundreds of dials, gauges, and levers. The pilot is constantly scanning the dials and gauges, monitoring not only the performance of the plane but also the environment. A great pilot can read those dials, know which levers to push and which knobs to turn to avoid an accident, and successfully navigate from where he is to where he wants to go. Without the dials, he will run out of fuel, stray off course, and ultimately crash and burn.

If I crawled into the cockpit of an F-16 and fired it up, there's a 100 percent probability that I would die. That's because I've got zero training and don't have a clue how to read any of the dials. But if I invested the time and energy needed to master every gauge and lever in that cockpit, and if I had a coach or a flight instructor train me, it would be a very different story.

You don't have to imagine an F-16. Piloting any plane requires training, and the faster you want to go or the worse the conditions, the more training you'll need.

As long as it's sunny outside, the plane is operating perfectly, it isn't too sophisticated, and you don't want to go very fast or very high, you can fly VFR, which stands for Visual Flight Rules. VFR means you look out the window of the cockpit and figure out where you are and proceed based on visual cues like highways, rivers, or towns. But the moment it gets cloudy outside and visibility turns murky, or the plane develops a slight problem, or you upgrade to a faster plane, then the pilot needs to know IFR, which stands for Instrument Flight Rules. IFR-rated pilots can fly very fast in extreme weather conditions by looking only at the instrument panel. VFR-rated pilots, on the other hand, are relegated to optimal weather conditions and a perfectly functioning plane.

Some business owners are like VFR-rated pilots trying to cope in an IFR environment. As economic conditions (weather) deteriorate and day turns into night, suddenly looking out the window simply will not suffice. These unsophisticated business owners wander off course, run out of fuel (cash), and make the six o'clock news (bankruptcy). All because they couldn't read the dials in the cockpit when the inevitable storm rolled in.

If you want to go fast or get big in business, make sure the business scoreboard of your cockpit can handle it, and practice reading those dials.

One of those dials, of course, is maximizing profits. Now, when you hear the word "maximize," your first instinct might be to think it means, "Get big!" But maximizing profits is not the same as hitting the sales or growth lever. **⊙⊷** The fastest path to profit maximization is reducing the drag of expenses, not building a bigger sales engine or pushing the growth throttle. Smart business owners will always pick the low-hanging fruit.

Suppose I have two businesses:

	Business A	Business B
Revenue	$100	$100
Expenses	$90	$90
Profits	$10	$10
Goal	⬆ Profits 30% to $13	⬆ Profits 30% to $13
Strategy	?	?

So far, these two businesses look exactly the same.

Let's suppose the management of Business A decides that their strategy to increase the profits from $10 to $13 (30 percent) is to increase their revenues from $100 to $125 (a 25 percent increase), which is aggressive for any business, regardless of the environment. Assuming that Business A enjoys the luxury of some economies of scale, this 25 percent increase in the growth of the top line (revenue) could result in the desired 30 percent growth on the bottom line (profits).

The management of Business B, on the other hand, has a different strategy. Business B has decided to take a hard look at *all* the expenses of the business, line by line, and ask the following question: ⚷ Do I *need* this or do I *want* it? If I want it, but don't need it, it's eligible to be reduced or eliminated. As Business B starts looking at each expense, a second question arises: What do I need it *for*?

Great question! Many years ago as I was reviewing the numbers on my monthly financial statements for one of our businesses, I noticed a significant aberration in one of the expense categories. Since my financial information is always presented in a trend format, the problem was easy to see. I immediately picked up the phone to talk to my general manager about this issue. When I asked how we could have had a sudden spike in this expense category, she told me, "Keith, that's just a cost of doing business."

I was stunned. I had no idea we had "costs of doing business." I thought we only had "investments." My accountants might have expenses and costs. As the business owner, I only have investments.

Think about it. Why are you in business? Why do you spend

money? 🔑 There are only two possible reasons, regardless of what business or industry you're in:

1. To keep the customers you have, or

2. To get new ones.

That's it.

🔑 Every dime I spend is an investment in keeping (and servicing) the customers I have or in getting new ones. Money spent that does not support one of these two outcomes is a waste.

Here is the great part of this lesson: 🔑 All investments earn a return and all returns can be measured. By measuring your success in attracting new customers, referrals, and repeat business, you can literally measure how effectively your money is being used. "Costs" and "expenses," on the other hand, are black holes. Money disappears into them, never to be seen again.

So, let's go back to our two businesses.

	Business A	Business B
Revenue	$125	$100
Expenses	$112	$87
Profits	$13	$13
Goal	⬆ Profits 30% to $13	⬆ Profits 30% to $13
Strategy	⬆ Revenue by 25% to $125	⬇ Expenses by 3.5% to $87

Business A's strategy was to grow the business, probably by ramping up the advertising, rebuilding the website, creating new brochures, blogging three times per day, tweeting two times per week, and adding one new salesperson. All of which is very exciting, takes a ton of work, costs money . . . and is highly unpredictable.

Business B had a different strategy. Looking closely at every expense—line by line, check by check, vendor by vendor—and thinking in terms of needs vs. wants and investments vs. costs, Business B was able to increase its profits 30 percent by cutting expenses by 3.5 percent . . . without growing revenues!

Let me say this another way: With a profit margin of 10 percent, every dollar reduction in expenses equates to a $10 increase in revenue without the need to find, close, and deliver on additional sales. Now that is business intelligence.

Of the thousands of businesses I have looked at over the past forty years, I have yet to see a business that wasn't wasting 8 to 10 percent of its revenue on stuff that made no difference. Put me in charge of your income statement and I'll whack 10 percent off your expenses in sixty days. Just like that. Increasing your revenues by 25 percent is a multi-month initiative at best. Reducing expenses by 5 to 10 percent is a sixty-day process at most. And the investment required to reduce your expenses is insignificant compared with the investment required to ramp up revenue.

⚷ Here is a formula for doubling your profits in the next sixty days. If your expenses are 90 percent of revenue (as they are for most small businesses), guess what happens when you eliminate 11 percent of your expenses? Your profits double! If your expenses are 85 percent of revenue, then reducing your expenses by 10 percent will drive profits up by 57 percent! Not too shabby for an afternoon's work.

Controlling expenses is typically relegated to the same "to-do" list as raking the leaves and returning an overdue library book. Big mistake! Sure, vacuuming up nickels, dimes, and quarters seems like it would be tedious and painful, but, man, is it profitable. ⚷ Reducing expenses is the easiest, fastest way to turbo-charge your financial results.

I have been using a strategy I call N.O.G. for twenty-five years. That stands for "No Overhead Growth." It's the mantra we have in all of our businesses: How do we grow top-line revenues and maintain or *reduce* our expenses? We can't do it perfectly, of course; it's a constant work in progress. But it's one of our primary profit-maximization strategies. In tough economic times, figuring out how to maintain profits with declining revenues is paramount.

The first step is to stop thinking of profits as money. The common-size analysis tool (thinking in terms of percentages) is a far more effective way of measuring. By using percentages, you can gauge if the business is doing comparatively better or worse than the year before with greater accuracy and speed. A second strategy is to use the per-unit analysis to compare your results in the current time period with prior time periods' results. Using either (or both) of these measurement strategies will enhance your ability to see the places where you're leaving money on the table and sabotaging your financial performance.

⚷ The fundamental strategy for maximizing profits is to optimize *before* you grow. Scaling a cancerous business simply means that you'll have a bigger tumor. The larger the tumor, the more life-threatening and difficult the surgery. First, eradicate the tumor, *then* get bigger. Grow the *efficiency*, not the *problem*.

Maximizing profits is only one of the critical dials in your business cockpit. Understanding how to read the fuel gauge to avoid running out of gas is another. It does no good to go faster only to burn through the gas sooner. In Chapter 10, I'll show you how to avoid an empty fuel tank and, more importantly, how to refill it mid-flight.

Chapter 10

Maximizing Cash Flow

Do you know the number one reason nine out of ten new businesses don't see their tenth birthday? It's not that their owners lack passion or drive. It's not that there's insufficient demand for their product or service. It's not that they aren't logging the hours, and it's certainly not because they aren't marketing and selling.

It's a cash thing.

⚷ Businesses fail when they run out of cash. Businesses fail because they can't pay their bills. A business cannot survive even a week without the oxygen of cash.

If you expect to keep the doors open, it's critical that you maximize cash and cash flow. So how do you maximize your cash flow so that your business doesn't become just another statistic in the business obituary column?

Let me repeat what I said in Chapter 6: ⚷ Not all cash is created equal. Cash can be generated or used in only three ways: Operations, Investing, and Financing. While all three are cash, only one of them is a result of running the business end of your business—and that's *operating* cash flow (or OCF). Sure, you can generate cash flow by selling your company car or your used computer (*investing* cash flow, or ICF) or you can borrow money from the bank or get your rich uncle to invest a few more dollars (*financing* cash flow, or FCF), but neither one of these are sustainable. There is a limit on how much "things and stuff" you own that can be sold and how much money you can borrow.

🔑 *To be sustainable, your business must produce positive cash flow from the <u>operations</u> of the business.*

When business owners start to confuse the sources of cash in their business, they're headed for trouble. Only operating cash flow tells the story of how *productive* management is at converting profits (theory) into cash (fact).

🔑 If you're unhappy with your operating cash flow, you have a total of five levers you can pull. Your income statement drives the first two:

1. Sell more.

2. Spend less.

Your balance sheet drives the last three:

3. Reduce accounts receivable days (the average length of time it takes your customers to pay you what they owe).

4. Reduce inventory days (the average length of time your inventory sits on your shelf before it is used or sold).

5. Increase accounts payable days (the average length of time it takes you to pay your bills).

That's all you get—just five levers. We all have to pay our bills. But we do have some say as to when we pay them. The longer you can extend your payables, the more OCF you'll have to run your business. Why would this be true? Because if you haven't paid your bills yet, you, not your vendors, have the cash.

What about receivables? If you haven't received the money yet, the cash is in your customer's bank account, not yours. The longer your customers owe you money for stuff they purchased but haven't paid for, the longer they have your cash (and you don't), which is bad for *your* operating cash.

Inventory is the other balance sheet category that directly affects operating cash. Unsold inventory reduces operating cash. The more stuff sitting in your warehouse and the longer it takes to sell it, the worse it is for your operating cash.

Part of solid business optics involves the calculations to convert the monetary/currency amount of receivables, inventory, and payables into *days outstanding*. CFO Scoreboard® performs all these calculations for you *and* displays your trends! It is a lot easier (and more meaningful) to see the impact of escalating receivables or inventory when the number is presented in *days* instead of dollars (currency).

🔑 If you want to drive your operating cash flow, it's mandatory you start measuring. Remember, *what gets measured is what gets managed. Measure results, change activities.* If you see your common size expense percentages (expenses as a percentage of revenues) starting to creep up, focus on expense-reduction strategies.

If your operating cash is suffering because of cash trapped on your balance sheet, here are several other strategies you could deploy:

RECEIVABLES

1. Set the customer's expectations upfront. This is an example of the conversation (which is very different from an invoice or written agreement) I would have with a new customer: "I am excited about doing this work for you. There is no question I will provide you with the product and service you want, and I will deliver it on time, as we agreed. However, I am not a bank, and I am not able to provide you with long-term financing. When I send a bill, it means the bill is due and I need to be paid. Typically, I have already paid the costs of providing the product to you and I cannot stay in business if you string me along. I do not want to have to beg for my money any more than you want to beg me to do the work. Can we have an ironclad agreement? I will do the work and I will do it on time, and in exchange, you agree to pay me within ten days of receipt of my bill. No runarounds, no delays, no checks-in-the-mail stuff. Agreed?"

2. ⚷ You get what you tolerate. What most business owners tolerate are customers who pay when it's convenient to the customer and not according to the agreement. You can bet your last nickel they pay their light bill on time, because if they don't, they're working in the dark. It does no good to have an agreement if you're unwilling to enforce it.

3. Be proactive with your customers. Call frequently and repeatedly. The squeaky wheel gets the grease.

4. Every one of your accounts receivable is someone else's accounts payable. There is a person in charge of accounts payable in every company with whom you do business. Send that person a $10 Starbucks card and a "thank you" for always being so great to you. It works!

5. Stop doing business with people who abuse you by not honoring the terms of your agreement.

6. Get a credit card backup from the customer, just in case their dog eats your invoice and they attempt to string you out.

Every time I talk about this topic, I always get pushback from business owners who will explain to me why their business is different. They do business with the government, or with health-care payers, or with some humongous business that abuses everyone. I understand. The question for you might not be how to fix it but rather how to improve it. Is there anything, I mean *anything*, you could do to knock a few days off the receivable days total? Good, then start doing that and improve your cash flow!

INVENTORY

1. Place smaller inventory orders and place your orders more frequently.

2. Negotiate with your suppliers on shipping and handling fees.

3. Renegotiate the price and terms of your inventory. Go out to bid. Talk to new suppliers who are aggressive in wanting your business.

4. Sell all the obsolete stuff and clean out the warehouse. Dust the shelves and start fresh.

5. Track your inventory closely to see what sells and what doesn't.

6. Stop buying stuff that doesn't sell and get rid of the stuff that hasn't sold.

7. Avoid letting your suppliers unilaterally stock your shelves. They get paid by the amount they stock, not the amount you sell.

8. Start monitoring the shrinkage. This is the inventory that never makes it to the cash register because either it is damaged or one of your customers (or employees) "borrows" something and forgets to tell you about it.

PAYABLES

1. Look at all payment agreements, and stretch your payment to the last day within the discount period or the last pre-penalty day.

2. Negotiate longer payment terms with your suppliers.

3. Pay bills one time per week and always pay before the penalty period.

4. Always avoid late charges.

5. Avoid disappointing your suppliers on payments.

Paying your bills on time (but not ahead of time) is simply good business. Besides, you will need a favor someday.

Since operating cash flow is the mother lode of business, here are four rules about operating cash flow that you should continuously measure (monthly, quarterly, and annually) and never forget:

1. 🔑 *Operating cash flow (OCF) should be positive.*

   Negative OCF means the business is losing cash from the operations of the business. A negative OCF means the sustainability of the business is in jeopardy because the business is paying its bills by:

   a. Dipping into savings.

   b. Selling assets like a vehicle or computer.

   c. Raising money from a third party, like a bank or an investor.

   d. Paying bills late.

   Sometimes, during a growth spurt for example, a healthy business might temporarily slip into negative OCF territory. This typically happens when a business grows very rapidly and has high inventory needs or large accounts receivable balances. This doesn't mean it's a broken business, but it should be the exception (a short-lived exception), not the rule. These instances usually don't last long, but they can be painful. When this happens, you must be very adept at juggling the cash.

2. ⚷ *Operating cash flow should be greater than profits.*

    This might sound strange at first glance, but it has to do with depreciation and amortization. On an income statement, not all expenses are cash expenses. Depreciation (the expensing of a *tangible* asset over the expected useful life of that asset) and amortization (the expensing of an *intangible* asset, patent, or goodwill over the expected useful life of that asset) are examples of expenses that reduce profits but have no impact on cash. Therefore, if your business has depreciation and/or amortization expenses, your profits should be smaller than your OCF. If your OCF is smaller than the profits, check the balance sheet categories we just discussed to find the disease that is consuming your cash and threatening your sustainability. Correct these cash drains immediately by reducing receivables and inventory and stretching out accounts payable.

3. ⚷ *Operating cash flow should be growing faster than profits.*

    If profits are up by 10 percent, OCF should increase by at least 10 percent. In a well-run business, OCF will be increasing at a greater percentage growth rate than profits. A business that makes less and less on more and more will eventually go broke. What we don't want to see is a business whose profits are going up but whose OCF is stagnant or declining. This is a business that is becoming less and less *productive* at converting profits into operating cash flow.

4. 🔑 *Operating cash flow is bigger than investing cash needs.*

    Said another way, OCF > ICF. A business whose operating cash flow is greater than its investment cash requirements is self-sufficient and does not have to rely on third-party financing. Management can spend its time running the business instead of preparing offering memorandums or knocking on doors to raise capital. Raising money is a full-time job and a major distraction from the operations of a business. There are some businesses (real estate and cable television, for example) that are capital intensive and require the purchase of tons of assets to grow or maintain the revenue of the business. These types of businesses will almost never achieve OCF that is greater than ICF needs, so they will always be raising money. Capital-intensive businesses consume investing cash in order to grow.

🔑 If operating cash flow exceeds investment cash needs, then the excess balance is *free cash flow*. Free cash flow is the amount of cash the owners can:

1. Reinvest in the business (buy more assets).

2. Use to repay debt.

3. Distribute to themselves as dividends, distributions, or compensation.

Remember *The Ultimate Blueprint for an Insanely Successful Business* we discussed in Chapter 6? Here is an enhanced "blueprint" including the concept of *free cash flow*:

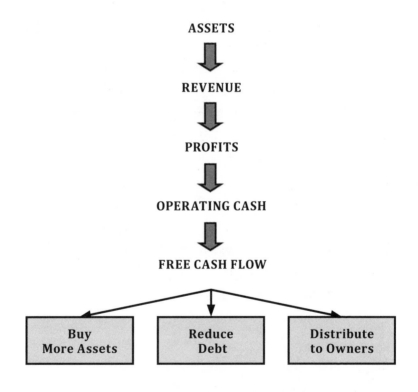

🗝 *Only cash can be reinvested back into the business, used to repay debt, or be distributed to the owners.*

In a good business, OCF will always exceed net income. In a

great business, operating cash flow exceeds investing cash flow needs, too. That's because a great business is able to self-fund. If your operating cash flow is $10,000 and your investment needs are $3,000, then you're able to fund your internal growth without relying on the generosity of strangers. Now that's a great business!

In this example, keep in mind that the amount of cash you, as the business owner, can distribute to yourself is the net $7,000, not the gross $10,000. It's one of the reasons I don't like the taxicab business. Let's say an average taxicab owner has OCF of $100,000 a year. But in order for a taxicab owner to stay in business, she has to spend $60,000 on a new car every year. Her free cash flow is the cash she generates from operating the taxicab ($100,000 of OCF) minus the cash she has to invest in purchasing a new car ($60,000 of ICF) every year. So while it may look like she's making $100,000, her free cash flow is only $40,000.

You might be thinking, "Keith, I'm not a taxicab driver. My company is making profits of $2,000,000 a year. How does this apply to me?" The size of a business is inconsequential. I advise, coach, mentor, and consult with companies across a very wide spectrum, and I've found that a business with profits of $5,000,000 typically has exactly the same core problems as a company with earnings of $100. They're both unaware of the distinction that profits are not cash, that not all cash is created equal, that their operating cash flow is MIA, and that they are burning cash while producing a theoretical profit! While the businesses may be operating on different scales or in different industries, they all have an undiagnosed tumor that is silently wrecking the business because they are not as *effective*, *efficient*, and *productive* as they could be.

Remember what I said: 🔑 The goal is to get rich, not big, and the way to get rich and stay rich is to maximize the profits and the operating cash flow that your business generates. I'll say it another way: 🔑 Getting big is a result of success. Success is not a result of getting big.

If your profits (or earnings) are going up, and your cash flow is going down, that's a red flag. It's what I call a "financial weed" in your business's garden. Financial weeds are typically visible only when the business owner converts raw accounting and bookkeeping data into usable business and financial optics. (I designed and built CFO Scoreboard® to do just that.) And if you do find a financial weed, that's a call to action.

🔑 Here is the best part about all the cash flow maximization strategies we've discussed: very small changes can have enormous ramifications for your cash flow. Depending on the size of your business, a three- to four-day swing in reducing receivable days, say, or increasing payable days can mean hundreds of thousands of dollars of additional cash in the bank *without increasing revenues*. Do them in combination and it is staggering how much incremental operating cash flow (and therefore cash in your bank account) you will generate. It is not uncommon for a business with as little as $1,000,000 in revenue to be able to improve its bank account by more than $100,000 in less than 90 days. How big is your business? You do the math.

🔑 One of the most frequently quoted sayings in the business world is, "Revenue is vanity . . . Profits are sanity . . . Cash is king." The reality is that not all cash is equal. Operating cash flow and free cash flow are the *true* kings of business. 🗝 In fact, I would say that Free Cash Flow is the fourth bottom line.

You will want to carefully examine the following chart to see all five levers, and the strategies and tactics, available to ramp up your OCF.

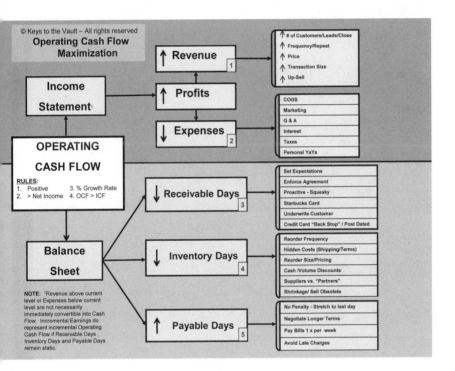

Chapter 11

Keeping Score

News flash: Your accounting report cards are for running your business, not paying your taxes!

This is a critical and massively misunderstood topic. Sadly, the vast majority of small business owners make the tragic mistake of attempting to keep score using the wrong accounting reporting methodology. And without the correct reporting system, you have no hope of ever running the business end of your business.

Without making this more complex than it needs to be or turning you into a bookkeeper, believe me when I say there is a right way and a wrong way to keep score. You have two options when it comes to the accounting methodology you use for your business: *cash accounting* or *accrual accounting*. If you attempt to keep score using the wrong accounting methodology, business optics and keeping score are the least of your problems. Attempting to get a handle on your I.Q. by stepping on the bathroom scale is a waste of time.

Cash accounting is a huge mistake, and unfortunately, it's the method most commonly used by most small business owners. ⚷ Accrual accounting is the correct and only way to keep score if you expect to have great business optics, make better decisions, and as a result, make more money.

I want to illustrate just how critical this distinction is. According to *Bloomberg*, there are over 9,000 publicly listed companies in the United States and approximately 63,000 worldwide. Guess how many of them use cash accounting? Zero! Not one. How do you think they got big? I promise you it wasn't by using the wrong yardstick. Success leaves clues!

Cash accounting records *only* those transactions in which actual cash changes hands. If it doesn't involve cash, cash accounting ignores the transaction until the cash is actually deposited or paid out. To my knowledge, there's only one business that is a *pure* cash business with no receivables, payables, or inventory. It operates totally on a cash basis for 100 percent of its transactions. The rest of us take credit cards, receive IOUs or checks from our customers, buy more inventory than we can sell in one month, and issue IOUs to our suppliers. If you happen to be in the crack cocaine business, you can keep using the cash method of accounting. The rest of us? We're going to rely on the accrual accounting method to accurately keep tabs on where we are and what's going on in our businesses.

⚷ Accrual accounting asks three questions: "Did you earn it? Do you owe it? Did you use it?" If the answer to any of these questions is "yes," then you record it. Cash accounting asks, "Did you spend some cash or collect some cash?" If you did, record it. If you didn't, don't.

Sometimes your business will make a sale (earn it) in January

but not collect the money until March. But you paid the light bill for January in January, and your employees all got paid in January for work done in January. Cash accounting would tell you to record the sale in March, which is when you actually received the cash. And cash accounting would tell you to record all your expenses when you wrote the checks for the electricity bill and the payroll, which was January. The problem is that you recorded *costs* in one month and the *revenue* associated with those expenses in a different month. You haven't matched the revenues and expenses to the same time period.
⚷ Matching is critical to measuring.

If you have several customers, for example, who delay paying you for a couple of months, it looks, on a cash-accounting basis, like you're really struggling on your income statement until the month that everyone pays and then you look like a hero. Accrual accounting, on the other hand, says that it is important to *match* the costs of generating or servicing a sale in the same time period as the sale was produced, not with the receipt or payment of cash.

Your business might place an extra-large order for inventory in January. Let's use an example of $9,000. In order to get really good terms, you might have to pay for all this inventory in cash in January. The reality is that you might sell or *use* the inventory purchased over the next three months at the rate of $3,000 per month. Cash accounting would tell you to record 100 percent of the inventory purchased as an "expense" or cost in January because you paid for it in January, which makes January profits look awful. In February and March, you didn't have to use more cash to buy additional inventory—because you had enough left over from the January purchase—so cash accounting would say there were no inventory costs or cost of goods sold in February and March, even though you actually used $3,000 of your inventory each month. With cash accounting, you look like you're going broke in January but in February and March you look like the reincarnation of Bill Gates.

☛ Matching the revenue or sale with the costs of producing or servicing that sale *in the same time period* is critical to accurately keeping score, and that's what accrual accounting does.

Since this is getting pretty technical, and I don't want to lose you, here is an easier example. Maybe your business owns a building. The property taxes and insurance are due in one lump sum payment every December. Suppose these two expenses total $12,000 for the entire year. You will certainly write the check in December for $12,000, and your cash will go down by $12,000 in December, but when did the expense *really* occur? Didn't it partially occur every month for the past 12 months? Accrual accounting would tell you to record 1/12 of $12,000 ($1,000/month) every month as an expense. Cash accounting would tell you to only record the taxes and insurance as an expense in the month that it was paid (December), regardless of when it was used or owed. In cash accounting you look great for eleven months out of the year, but in the month of December you look incompetent.

Accrual accounting is the only accounting system that gives you an accurate reading of your *true* financial performance based on matching the revenue *earned* with the expenses *incurred*, regardless of when you collected the revenue or paid the expenses.

In true cash accounting, there are no receivables or payables. There is no inventory. In fact, there is no cash flow statement, which is probably why you have never seen one. Your check register has become your income statement. Deposits have been recorded as revenues and checks written are expenses. This is as absurd as it is deadly. To measure your results and correct the underlying activities so that you can be more effective, efficient, and productive, you must use the correct accounting methodology: accrual accounting.

So why do businesses use cash accounting? Partly because it's easier to grasp. Most business owners don't understand the concept of profits as a theory nor realize that profits can't be spent. They think that if there is a $ or £ or € symbol in front of a number, it must be cash. It's not. Bizarrely, they do understand having profits but no cash to meet payroll or make their note payment to the bank; they just can't see why this is happening because of the cash accounting issue.

Many times, small business accountants are more concerned about filing the tax return at year-end than presenting your financial information in a format that provides you with the optics to actually make good decisions and run the business end of your business. These accountants will attempt to convince you that cash accounting is less expensive and easier to understand, and they are right if all you are concerned about is filing a tax return. But you will never hear a competent accountant tell you that cash accounting is more accurate for financial optics.

The reality is that the government is partially responsible for this whole mess concerning cash vs. accrual accounting, because in most countries, the government expects you to pay your taxes based on *cash* received and disbursed, not on the true profits of your business. On the other hand, the government is also largely responsible for getting most business owners to even keep financial records of any sort. I seriously doubt the majority of small and medium-sized business owners would even bother if there were no income tax reporting requirements.

When you stop to think about it, having three report cards really is important. They are each designed to do entirely different things:

- A balance sheet keeps track of your things and stuff and whether you owe or own your things and stuff.

- An income statement keeps track of whether or not the revenue (sales) of your business exceeds the costs (expenses)—regardless of the timing of cash changing hands—and therefore whether your business is theoretically profitable.

- A cash flow statement tracks where cash is generated and used in a business.

I am warning you that it is highly likely your accountant or bookkeeper will attempt to persuade you that cash accounting is fine. They might try to convince you that the cost of switching is egregious. It's not. This argument is never made by a true business accountant.

There are four primary requirements to convert from cash to accrual accounting. My accounting friends are dying to lengthen this list, but the following four requirements below will get you started.

1. Match the revenue (sales) and the costs (expenses) of those revenues to the time period in which you earn it, owe it, or use it.

2. Record the revenue in the time period in which it occurs (earn it), which means you will track and record your accounts receivable on the balance sheet.

3. Record your expenses in the time period in which they occur (owe it), which means you will track and record your accounts payable on the balance sheet.

4. Record your inventory purchased on the balance sheet and the amount of inventory used in each time period on the income statement as a cost of goods sold (COGS).

Do not be tempted to hit the button in your QuickBooks or MYOB accounting software that lets you automatically convert from cash to accrual accounting. That button does no good if you haven't followed the four rules outlined above. Better yet, don't worry about this accounting stuff. Go out and hire someone (part-time is better than nothing) who understands the importance of measuring and business optics so that you can run the business end of your business.

If you need accounting support on a project or full-time basis, let us know. We can refer you to highly competent people who can do this for you.

Chapter 12

Three Sets of Books?

 The reality of the business world is that every business owner should have a minimum of two sets of books or accounting reports. One set of financial reports will not cut it. I sometimes recommend business owners keep *three* sets of books, and I'll explain why in a moment. Whether you choose to keep two or three sets, your different sets of accounting reports should be kept separate and distinct, because what goes in one won't necessarily go in another.

As you learned in the last chapter, the first set of books is based on accrual accounting. An accurate accrual accounting-based report card is the only way to go if you expect to be able to accurately measure your results and subsequently reverse engineer the numbers to figure out which activities need to change to create optimal and sustainable success. (This is the definition of *business optics*!)

Then there are the financial records you need to keep for the federal government, in order to pay your income taxes. What you have to realize is that the government does not want an accurate reflection of what happened in your business. For example, in the United States, the government stipulates that half your meals are nondeductible. So you might have spent forty bucks on a steak, but you can only deduct twenty as an expense for tax purposes. There are also limits on your charitable and health-care deductions.

Here is another significant distinction: Most of us have had the experience of getting to the end of the year and receiving a big check from one of our customers. Maybe the client has owed you money for the past couple of months, and they finally pay you $20,000 on December 30, probably because they want the deduction in the current year so they can reduce *their* taxes. If you are like most business owners, even though you made the sale and *earned* this money back in August, you choose to delay depositing the money until January 2 of next year, thus reducing your own taxes this year. Perhaps you write a few checks on December 29 for January bills that aren't even due yet. These are bills that should be paid in January or February of next year, but you write the checks in December. Sometimes you haven't even received the invoice yet, but you write the check anyway. Why do we do this? Because *the government uses a modified cash accounting* treatment. If you didn't actually receive it (deposit it) this year, then you don't have to pay taxes on it this year. And if you paid for it this year, great—you get to deduct it from your profits this year and therefore pay less in taxes this year.

🔑 The government does not care when we *earned, owed,* or *used* it, only when we received or disbursed the cash.

🔑 The accounting we do for the government has nothing to do with the accrual accounting we should use to run our businesses. So that gives us two sets of financial records: accrual accounting and tax (or government) accounting. This is where it gets tricky and the third set of books might come into play.

Let me be clear: I'm not advocating a third set of books. On the other hand, having advised and consulted literally thousands of business owners has convinced me that most small or medium-sized business owners delay deposits, accelerate expenses, and pad their tax returns with deductions that are primarily personal expenses—their "ya-ya"—that have zero business justification.

As one of my mentors told me years ago, "Keith, facts don't cease to exist just because you ignore them." He was right. The vast majority of small-to-medium-sized businesses play some kind of game with the government to minimize their tax bill.

If you choose to play this game with your taxes, you must not allow this financial hanky-panky to contaminate your actual monthly—100 percent business-related—*accrual* accounting reports. It is mandatory that you have at least one set of books that are totally accurate and that reflect what actually happened in your business on a purely business basis in the time period in which money was earned, owed, or used (accrual). The second set of books are the tax accounting required by the government. Ordinarily, the tax-accounting treatment would not be that difficult; however, we complicate things when we decide to minimize our tax bill by writing off purely personal items.

This is where the third set of books comes in. I don't mean an entirely new set of QuickBooks, Peachtree, MYOB, or whatever accounting system you use, but I do mean that you should keep the personal expenses you intend to claim as a business expense in a separate category from your bona fide business expenses in your monthly accrual accounting report cards.

If you are tempted to write off last year's vacation to New Zealand as market research, or if your college-age children miraculously find their way onto your company payroll (siphoning off some profits from your own higher tax bracket into their lower tax bracket), or if your spouse receives a diamond bracelet for Christmas and you simultaneously declare her employee of the month, you are creating a nightmare with your ability to accurately measure your financial performance.

⚷ One of the biggest mistakes small business owners make is the commingling of business and personal funds. Money seems to flow effortlessly between the two with little thought of how it is going to affect anything other than taxes. Big mistake! In larger businesses and publicly held companies, when management starts helping themselves to company money or the books get cooked to report false earnings, somebody goes to prison.

I am chairman of the board for 120 business owners. Each Board is comprised of fifteen members. And each of our Boards meets several times per year in two- or three-day sessions to work on each other's businesses, review financial reports, and provide each other with optics, advice, and insight. To say these meetings are intense would be an understatement.

A couple of years ago, a new member presented his company and its problems at one of these meetings. His story was that his business wasn't performing very well financially, despite the fact that his revenues were almost $2 million per year. He was low on cash every month, struggled to meet payroll, appeared to be barely breaking even, and was stressed beyond imagination. His proposed solution was to turbo-charge his business and ramp up revenues to $3 million per year. I asked for his financial reports, and, sure enough, he was teetering on being broke.

I couldn't see the root of the problem, however, because of the way his financial statements were presented. I asked him to show us how much he was pulling out of the business for his personal salary and ya-ya. One hour later, we had reconstructed his numbers, and, to his surprise, he was dragging $750,000 a year. His business was performing quite well, but he was suffocating it by having his business pay for his personal consumption. An even bigger problem was that he wasn't aware of the magnitude of personal expenses that had crept into his business over the years because he never bothered to request an accurate set of financial statements. Things like the pool repair, yard service, life insurance on his spouse, the maid, vacations, dining out, gas, repairs, and insurance for the cars he had the business buy for his three kids . . . the list goes on. Ignorance was not bliss.

If you're going to play with fire, at least have enough sense to avoid burning down the house. If you choose to play this game—which is not my advice—here is how you could do it: Create two large categories of expenses. The first one is called "above-the-line expenses." These are the legitimate expenses required to operate your business. Your personal expenses are recorded in a separate category called "below the line." When you are doing your measuring and financial analysis, record your personal expenses below your *business net income line* so you can easily see how well your business is performing both before and after the personal stuff. When you are reporting your taxes, merge or combine the "above-the-line" and "below-the-line" expenses into a single chart of accounts, file your tax return, and hold your breath.

Just so that you're aware, your balance sheet and cash flow statement will both be screwed up as a result of the personal ya-ya expenses you run through your income statement, and, of course, this further complicates the process of measuring. It's hard to know how much you really weigh if you're lugging around a boulder in your pocket.

Be extremely careful when you start messing around with these sets of books. Think about what would happen if someone were to monkey around with the altimeter of an F-16. If the plane is at sea level, but the gauge shows an altitude of 500 feet, chances are good that even the best pilot will crash when he tries to land.

Regardless of whether you decide a third set of books is right for you, having the first two sets of books is mandatory. You should have one set of books that is precisely accurate—your accrual accounting books (without any shenanigans)—so that you can accurately measure your performance, and another set of books where you record your expenses for the federal government using their definition of cash accounting.

There's an added benefit of an accurate set of books if you decide to exit your business. It is difficult to remember exactly which expenses were personal three years after the fact. If you get it wrong, you risk devaluing your business because the expenses were inflated for tax purposes, which causes the profits (and therefore, the exit value) to be understated.

If your business is valued at a five times multiple of earnings and you forget about $100,000 of personal expenses, your exit value has just been whacked by $500,000.

Lest you think I'm leading you astray here, every major company has two sets of books—IBM, Microsoft, Apple, GE. They've all got one that's accrual accounting and another one for tax purposes. Most small business owners, on the other hand, have only one set of books: the cash accounting one for the tax man. And that's a mistake.

You've got to have one set of books that's accurate, one set of books for the tax man, and then if you want to play the "Enron" game, you'll need a third.

Chapter 13

KPIs vs. Critical Drivers

In the typical economic cycle, the time period from trough to peak is about ten years. Ever wonder why more than 90 percent of businesses fail in ten years? Because most businesses survive only as long as the economy is on their side.

Any idiot can make money when the sun is shining, the wind is at their back, and the tide is rising. Just look at all the money made during the dot-com boom in the late 90s or the real estate riches from 2003–2007. The vast majority of people who made money riding these waves gave it all back when the economy flipped upside down.

⚷ If you can only be successful when the environment is helping, you are doomed to fail, because the only constant in business is change.

Acquiring the skills and tools required for sustainability is paramount. And creating sustainable success means you know what to do in bad times and good.

We've talked a lot about the importance of measuring and how it's the only way to get the optics required to make good decisions and thereby create sustainable business success. So far, we have concentrated on a few of the *key performance indicators* or KPIs as they are sometimes called. Revenue ÷ Assets or OCF ÷ Profits are examples of KPIs. No question these are powerful tools, but the only problem with them is they are like bathroom scales. They tell you what has happened after the fact but are not predictive about what needs to change to create different results in the future. Business optics is fundamentally about KPIs. But if you want a PhD in measurement, if you want to amp your level of sophistication and permanently change your business game, you must look at critical drivers as well.

☛ Think of KPIs as *effects* and critical drivers as *causes*. If KPIs are your cholesterol, a critical driver is your diet.

The size of your revenue might be the KPI, but if you happen to be in a business that has a sales pipeline, for example, then what you did three months ago has serious implications for your results this month. Perhaps your business is affected by the size of each transaction, the number of speeches you gave, the commissions per sale, or the number of cold calls made. Any of these could be a critical driver for the revenue of your business.

Most business owners make the mistake of only measuring KPIs when they could, and should, be taking preemptive action by creating and measuring critical drivers, too. Critical drivers and KPIs are not mutually exclusive. You should never rely on just one or the other. The basics are KPIs. Critical drivers put your measuring, analysis, and performance on steroids.

☛ To determine your critical drivers, ask yourself this question: "When I have a bad month financially, what happened that shouldn't have happened or what should have happened that didn't happen?" Chances are that several things on this list are critical drivers of your business.

Regardless of the industry or business you're in, you'll only have three to five *critical* drivers. What they are will vary significantly from business to business, but any time you have a bad month financially, only a few things could have caused it. And none of them will be that somebody left the light on in the janitor's closet one night. These critical drivers are the *causes* of your business's results that you need to measure on a weekly or even a daily basis.

Executing, measuring, and correcting these critical driver activities on a consistent basis will ensure you never have a nasty surprise when you look at your accounting report cards at the end of the month. It's simply cause and effect.

☛ Any time the effect you want is missing, so is the cause. Manage the cause, and the effect takes care of itself.

An added benefit of identifying great critical drivers for your business tool belt is that you can course-correct daily instead of waiting until the fifteenth of the following month to see your financial results and measure your KPIs. A huge problem for business owners is the lag between a faulty decision or a wrong activity and the measurement of the results. Knowing and measuring your robust critical drivers solves this problem forever. Catch the errant activity or aberrations early before they become a problem and you'll have fewer problems.

Set, communicate, and measure the critical drivers, and you'll achieve superior results.

🔑 Set aside your Thinking Time to:

1. Develop the performance standards—the benchmarks and hurdles—for each critical driver.

2. Communicate those critical driver standards to your team.

3. Set the rewards and consequences around the attainment of these critical drivers.

4. Measure, report, and correct the critical driver execution on a daily basis.

You will be stunned at the execution and consistency your team produces.

Chapter 14

The Ultimate Goal

Let's raise our level of thinking from business owner to that of the board of directors. ⚿ The ultimate goal of being in business is not just the pursuit of revenues or profits or even cash. It's to *maximize the value* of the business over the long term.

A massive benefit of optimizing and maximizing the profits or earnings of your business is what it does to your exit value. Eliminating wasteful or pimped expenses of $50,000 not only adds $50,000 of additional profits to your bottom line—and your bank account—each and every year, it could increase your exit value by $250,000 or more. Now that is some serious value creation. But before you get too excited, it is critical for you to know that the size of your profits is just one factor in determining the value of your business.

⚿ The value of a business is directly tied to the size, predictability, sustainability, and growth rate of its earnings.

Businesses sell for a multiple of their earnings. The size of the multiple is fairly standard within an industry but varies widely between industries. Selling a dental practice might bring a multiple of one times earnings. A car wash on the other hand might sell for a multiple of five to seven times earnings. A cable television company would sell for twelve to thirteen times earnings. Why the wide variations? It all has to do with the predictability, sustainability, and growth rate of the earnings being valued:

Value

=

Earnings × Multiple

(adjusted for the Growth Rate and Risk)

	Business A Earnings	Business B Earnings
Year 1	$10K	$100K
Year 2	$25K	$75K
Year 3	$50K	$50K

Think about it this way. Let's say I show you Business A, whose earnings have gone from $10,000 to $25,000 to $50,000 over the past three years. Then I show you Business B, in the exact same industry, whose earnings have gone from $100,000 to $75,000 to $50,000 over the past three years. They both have $50,000 of earnings in the current year. Yet if I asked you which business is more valuable, all other things being equal, you would tell me Business A. Because Business A's earnings are increasing, its "multiple" will be greater, to account for its superior earnings growth rate.

The greater a business's past or projected earnings growth rate, the greater its perceived value. However, in determining the value of a business, earnings and growth rates are always adjusted for the *risk* and probability of those earnings continuing in the future (*predictability* and *sustainability*).

Suppose I told you that Business B (the one with declining earnings) had 1,000 customers and that no single customer accounted for more than 1 percent of the revenue. Suppose Business A (the one with increasing earnings) only had five customers and one of those customers accounted for 60 percent of the revenues and profits.

Now which one is more valuable? It's hard to know since a business with this kind of customer concentration has tremendous exposure. If Business A loses its biggest customer, it will be seriously crippled or out of business. This concentration risk in Business A would require a downward adjustment to its earnings multiple as compared with Business B's multiple.

This is why business owners make a grave and often deadly mistake when they focus maniacally on how big their company is or how fast it's growing, both of which are typically measured by revenue.

I am not saying revenue or revenue growth rates are immaterial or have no impact on value. They do. Revenue growth is often a reflection of marketplace acceptance or competitive strength. But exclusively focusing on the top line, while ignoring the investment required to produce those revenues, and the risk factors that could disrupt or discontinue those revenues and ultimately profits, is shortsighted and deadly.

Risks come in all shapes and sizes: Lawsuits, key suppliers going broke, a key executive falling ill, bad press, escalating competition, and increasing interest rates are all possibilities. ⚷ *In many ways, maximizing business value is, ironically, about minimizing risk.* Anybody who ignores risk won't be in business long.

So how do you minimize the risks? While there are no foolproof methods, the best advice I have is to do three things. And all of them require Thinking Time:

1. 🔑 Identify the risks. No risk can be controlled or minimized unless it has first been identified. Think about and make a list of the things that could go wrong. A coach or adviser is critical at this juncture, because most of us can't realistically see the "gotchas" that are looming on the horizon. In fact, the single biggest risk most of us face involves the *assumptions* we make about the future. Assumptions are fatal. What we call facts are usually nothing more than wishful thinking and irrational exuberance—optimism on steroids. I heard once that what most people call thinking is nothing more than rearranging preexisting prejudices. I agree.

2. 🔑 Think about the probability of each risk occurring and the associated cost of each risk in the event it does occur. Not all risks have an equal probability of occurring or an equal cost in the event of an occurrence. The likelihood of your best salesperson quitting is probably different from the probability of your source code being accidentally erased. Furthermore, the cost associated with the salesperson quitting is probably different from the cost of losing your source code. Think about probability *and* cost.

3. ⚷ Identify and rank the ten highest probability risks that also have the largest potential financial cost. Immediately begin working on controlling, minimizing, mitigating, and managing two things: 1) The likelihood of each risk occurring, and 2) If it does occur, the monetary cost. You want to contain the exposure and minimize the costs.

Certainly optimizing and maximizing profits and cash flow are critical components of value. The purpose of this book has been to highlight and emphasize the strategies and techniques available to you to do that. And this book would be incomplete without simultaneously advising you on the discipline of making sure those profits and cash flows are predictable and sustainable long into the future.

No business owner should have sleepless nights. But if you find yourself wide-awake at 3 a.m., the only problem worth worrying about is, "What could disrupt my future stream of earnings?" These are the risks that will destroy the value of your business and make you obsolete.

Chapter 15

Introducing CFO Scoreboard®

You and I both know businesses do not run themselves. Somebody has to make the business and financial decisions. ⚷ Anyone who tries to run their business without measuring, financial optics, and a scoreboard is assuming they can successfully fly their business by the seat of their pants.

I'll say it a different way: Anyone who isn't serious about getting the best business and financial optics available is not serious about improving their business. We must have better optics if we expect to make better decisions. What you can't see can kill you.

I designed and built CFO Scoreboard® because most business owners are one wrong financial decision away from disaster. CFO Scoreboard® takes the brain damage out of understanding the numbers by giving business owners the financial measurements and business optics required to run the business end of their business. CFO Scoreboard® is a business owner's scoreboard, not an accounting "dashboard."

As Warren Buffett has said: "If you can't read the scoreboard, you don't know the score. If you don't know the score, you can't tell the winners from the losers." I'll take what Buffett said one step further: You can't tell the winners from the losers if you don't even have a scoreboard.

Accounting financial statements are *not* a scoreboard; they do not provide business optics because that is not what they were designed to do. They don't display your financial information in a way that will help you identify and diagnose underlying problems, prescribe remedial solutions, or prioritize your focus so that you can maximize your profits and cash flow.

Accountants typically prepare monthly financial statements and tax returns. Chief Financial Officers, or "CFOs," convert the accounting into strategic, executable business optics so that management has the visibility and clarity to make great decisions and avoid dumb mistakes.

This is where CFO Scoreboard® comes in. The power of CFO Scoreboard® is that it was built for nonfinancial business owners who don't want to get a degree in accounting or an MBA from Harvard or hire dozens of financial engineers to understand the numbers and get great decision-making optics. The people who use the CFO Scoreboard® want the optics and clarity without the brain damage.

CFO Scoreboard® does *not* replace your accounting system or your accountant. But it does import (no data entry!) and analyze your financial statements and help you make sense of them.

- We convert all that accounting mumbo jumbo into usable business optics so that you can actually see what is going on with your business, where the problems are, and what to do about them.

- We show you easy-to-digest reports and graphs that explain, in plain English, what's *really* going on in your business, what you're doing well, where you could improve, and how much it's costing you to ignore the problems.

- We crunch the numbers so you don't have to, and then we tell you what those numbers mean and how they are affecting *your* business's profits and operating cash flow.

- We extract the most important metrics from your accounting information, do the critical comparisons and trends, identify the problems, and tell you exactly what to do about them.

When you boil it down, you don't really care about adjusting journal entries, debits and credits, trial balances, and all that accounting stuff. What you want is a business tool that will help you do four primary things:

1. ⚷ Find and plug the profit leaks so you can maximize profitability.

2. ⚷ Find and plug the cash flow drains so you can put more money in your bank account.

3. ⚷ Have an early warning system to alert you to financial problems that could wreck your business if left uncorrected.

4. 🔑 Prioritize your activities so that you can avoid confusing breaking a sweat with productivity.

CFO Scoreboard® does for business owners what an MRI and CT scan for doctors: We give you the optics so you can see the hidden, but deadly, diseases that are sabotaging your profits, cash flow, and financial performance.

🔑 The most important financial decision you will ever make is not how to make money—it's how to keep it, how to grow it, and how to maximize it. That's why we built CFO Scoreboard®.

At CFO Scoreboard®, we have one outcome:

🔑 If you get better optics, you make better decisions. If you make better decisions, you make more money. It's that simple.

Check out our website (www.cfoscoreboard.com). Take the tour and watch some of our videos to get better acquainted with the power of CFO Scoreboard®. Using CFO Scoreboard® **will** change the way you do business and will put money in your jeans. I guarantee it.

Chapter 16

Getting Started

60-DAY CFO PLAN

When a business owner or management team gets serious about running the business end of their business, hires a CFO, or retains professional CFO support from a business adviser, I have found there are six major financial priorities and six major business-risk priorities that must be analyzed and managed on an ongoing basis to create a sustainable business. If I were you, I would use these chapters as the template to help get started and to know where to focus my attention.

The Big 6: Financial Optics

1. **Cash**: Everything stops when a business runs out of cash. Unlike most other situations a business might encounter, cash is a problem that is almost impossible to fix with duct tape. Kind of like oxygen . . . when it's

gone, you are in a state of extreme emergency and very soon thereafter, death. Your top priorities when you begin running the business end of your business are three things, and they are all about cash:

a. **Cash Balances:** Examine your monthly cash balances (found on your monthly balance sheets) for the last eighteen to twenty-four months to determine whether this number is growing or declining.

b. **Cash Sources:** You know from Chapter 10 that not all cash is created equal and that cash can be generated or used from three different activities:

- Operations

- Investing

- Financing

Your accountant should be able to supply you with your historical cash flow information in a "Direct" Cash Flow Statement, but just in case they haven't, CFO Scoreboard® automatically provides you with the exact optics on your historical monthly cash flow performance (we automatically calculate, for all time periods, your cash flow statements from the balance sheet and income statement you upload into CFO Scoreboard®). You must know which activities are either producing or using cash—specifically whether your cash flow is a result of selling goods and services ("O" cash), buying or selling assets ("I" cash), or borrowing or repaying money to your financiers ("F" cash).

If operating cash is the problem, here is a quick refresher on the five levers in your business's cockpit which can create cash flow leaks and inefficiencies:

- Revenue   ↓
- Expenses   ↑
- Receivables ↑ ┐
                ├— Other Current Assets ↑
- Inventory   ↑ ┘
- Payables & Current Liabilities ↓

Many times, a cash problem can be caused by spending too much money on property, plant, or equipment. Delaying, curtailing, or spreading the timing of future capital expenditures can help resolve a cash crisis. A corollary strategy would be to sell some of your unproductive or unused property, plant, and equipment to help alleviate a cash shortfall.

Financing cash problems are usually caused by a loan repayment schedule that is out of sync with the business's ability to generate cash and service the debt. A loan agreement was negotiated that was overly optimistic and now the business finds itself unable to meet its debt-service commitments. Renegotiating with the bank or finding a replacement lender can sometimes solve this crisis, although you and I both know banks love to loan you an umbrella when the sun is shining, but the instant it clouds up, they get very stingy, and if it is actually raining, forget about it. On the other hand, sometimes financing cash can be the solution for an "O" cash or "I" cash problem, especially if the cash problem is a result of rapid growth.

c. **Cash Burn Rate:** Knowing exactly how much fuel you have, how fast it is being consumed, and how long until you run out is critical information you must forecast to make informed decisions about your business. Looking backward at historical sources and uses of cash to understand whether the problem is operating, investing, or financing is the starting point, but to truly understand the cash position of your business, you must estimate how much total fuel you have in the gas tank and, at your anticipated rate of consumption, how much time is remaining before you run out.

🔑 A Rolling 13-Week Cash Forecast provides you with the CFO optics required for a thorough understanding of the business's future cash needs and is the single most important strategy for any business experiencing, or wanting to avoid, a cash crisis. This is the tool I have used for the past forty years to manage and turn around businesses in trouble. You should see Appendix A for a review and example of a Rolling 13-Week Cash Forecast.

2. ⚷ **Accounting Practices:** Most small businesses get started with cash accounting and, despite their growth, continue to use this accounting methodology. As you now know from Chapter 11, this is an incredibly bad idea! The cash accounting problem, with its wild monthly swings, is one of the primary reasons I created CFO Scoreboard® with monthly, short-term (trailing three months), and long-term (trailing twelve months) trend lines. These longer trend lines also support businesses which have either seasonality or cyclical characteristics.

Cleaning up the accounting includes recording receivables, inventory, and payables as they occur and matching the correct time period based on when something is earned, owed, or used.

Furthermore, for businesses that have subsidized the owner's personal expenses to minimize taxes, identifying and breaking out the owners "ya-ya" expenses into a "below-the-line" treatment will optimize the optics and analysis of the business's true profitability (Chapter 12). CFO Scoreboard® includes the flexibility to segregate

your owner's expenses and analyze your business before
and after owner's expenses.

3. **⚷ Profits:** A primary indicator of the viability and
sustainability of a business model is the profitability of
the business. The monthly and trailing trend line over
the past several years is critical to understanding the
financial dynamics of a business and whether or not
the business model is viable, improving, or declining.
These profitability calculations should be performed
on a monetary, common size, and "per-unit" basis
(Chapter 9).

4. **⚷ Profit Margin:** The profit margin of a business
(Profits ÷ Revenue) is the key metric to measure a business owner's ability to control expenses. If profit margins are declining, it is a perfect opportunity for you to
identify the expense structure (i.e., COGS, Variable,
Fixed, G&A, Marketing & Sales) trend lines. Once the
problem category has been identified, you must dig
deeper to find the specific expenses that are causing the
profit erosion. The best two tools for this analysis are
common sizing and "per-unit" analysis of all expenses
on an income statement (Chapter 5).

5. **⚷ Revenue:** Understanding the revenue sources and
trends from the past several years is vital for any CFO.
This analysis should include trends, seasonality, cycli-
cality, and "one-time" events (i.e., the loss of a major
customer). Knowing the direction of revenue (growth
or decline) and the percentage rate of movement is

critical to understanding a business's future HR, capital expenditures, cash, and financing requirements.

6. 🖩 **Return on Assets:** The word "Return" can be defined two different ways: Profits or Operating Cash Flow. You will want to monitor and maximize both.

Profits ÷ Assets is the fundamental measure of a business's ability to convert assets into profits. OCF ÷ Assets is the ultimate measurement of a business's success. Measuring the trend line of these relationships is also critical to understanding and having optics on a business's financial condition. A business which is experiencing a deterioration of its Return on Assets trend line is in jeopardy. For businesses that do not have significant assets on the balance sheet, an alternative definition of assets is "employees" or "payroll dollars," i.e., Profit per Employee or Profit per Payroll Dollar (Chapter 8).

Return on Assets, in which *return* is defined as *profits*, can be expressed in the form of two ratios multiplied together:

$$\frac{\text{Revenue}}{\text{Assets}} \times \frac{\text{Profits}}{\text{Revenue}} = \frac{\text{Profits}}{\text{Assets}} = \textbf{Return on Assets}$$

Measuring and "trend-lining" both the *effectiveness* (Revenue ÷ Assets) and *efficiency* (Profits ÷ Revenue) are mandatory for understanding and diagnosing the underlying financial issues of a business.

This ratio model can be expanded to determine the *productivity* of asset conversion into operating cash flow (OCF).

$$\frac{\text{Revenue}}{\text{Assets}} \times \frac{\text{Profits}}{\text{Revenue}} \times \frac{\text{OCF}}{\text{Profits}} = \frac{\text{OCF}}{\text{Assets}}$$

Said another way:

$$\text{Effectiveness} \times \text{Efficiency} \times \text{Productivity} = \frac{\text{OCF}}{\text{Assets}}$$

Business and financial optics require more than a familiarity with the raw numbers. The growth rate of these numbers is also a great predictor of potential problems. In a well-run business

- The percentage growth rate for operating cash flow should be greater than the percentage growth rate of profits.

- The profits percentage growth rate should be greater than the revenue percentage growth rate.

- The revenue percentage growth rate should be greater than the assets percentage growth rate (regardless of assets defined as number of employees, payroll dollars, or balance sheet figures).

Measuring absolute numbers is good; measuring and comparing growth rates is mastery (Chapter 6).

The Big 6: Business Risks

All businesses have risks, which is simply another way of saying something could go wrong. Some risks are identifiable by studying a business's financial statements (which is what CFO Scoreboard® is designed to do). Some risks are embedded in the structure or framework of the business and are hard to identify by looking only at the numbers. The following are the six essential "non-financial-statement" risks a CFO must address (and continue to monitor) to determine a business's financial exposure and ensure sustained success:

1. **⚷ Concentration Risk:** A business that produces $50,000,000 of profits is not necessarily a healthy business. If it has 10,000 customers and one of those customers accounts for 75 percent of its revenue and profits, this business is in serious jeopardy of failing. This is called concentration risk, and it happens when the business is too reliant on a single customer, supplier, distribution channel, account receivable, referral source, strategic partner, IT, employee, or owner. Another way of describing concentration risk is single-point-of-failure risk, meaning that if only one thing goes wrong, Humpty Dumpty can hit the concrete.

   Many founders of a business are comfortable with this kind of risk, until it occurs, because they know the people or companies involved and usually have years of experience of nothing going wrong. Typically these risks are tolerated on the basis of wishful thinking and

misguided assumptions, neither of which are particu-
larly useful for creating a *sustainably* successful business.

What they fail to appreciate is how these kinds of risks
expose the business to instant extinction in the event of
an occurrence, regardless of how rare it is. Furthermore,
concentration risk destroys exit values because most
buyers are uncomfortable with concentration risks, and
therefore ratchet the purchase price down or simply
pass on the deal. For most small businesses, the owner
is the most significant single-point-of-failure risk,
which explains their low exit valuations.

2. **⚷ Sustainability Risk:** What could disrupt the *future
stream of earnings*? This question cuts right to the heart
of risk analysis and is an extremely important question
for all owners and CFOs to think about. Earnings are
a result of revenues minus expenses, so the question I
am really asking is this: What could cause revenues to
tumble or expenses to escalate?

3. **⚷ Business Model Risk:** A business model is the
structure of how a business makes money and whether
or not the amount made is adequate to compensate
the investors for the risks they take. Embedded into
this definition are lots of unseen but vital assumptions
about the target market, pricing, competition, qual-
ity of products, distribution channels, performance
guarantees, asset acquisition and allocation, staffing
requirements, capital structure, etc. All business models

are subject to both internal and external pressures that will require you to bend and sometimes break your business model to remain competitive and relevant in the marketplace. Understanding the threats and weaknesses of your business model is imperative to creating a sustainable business.

4. **⚷ External Risk:** All businesses operate in an environment; therefore, they are subject to external risks. Something can always go wrong and often these bad things are not only external to the business but also things we have zero control over. External risks might include your competition, a hatchet job by the crew of *60 Minutes*, a regulatory change, China's GDP slowing down, interest rates skyrocketing, or a repeat of the 2008 economic meltdown. Some of these risks might be manageable but many more are uncontrollable. Whether the risk is internal or external, manageable or uncontrollable, it is vital that you identify these risks early on and keep your eye on them. Knowing where the gasoline is stored prior to the fire is critical to preventing the building from exploding in the event of an ill-conceived match.

5. **⚷ Leverage Risk:** When businesses borrow money, the underlying emotion is optimism. More often than not, the money is originally borrowed to facilitate some growth opportunity the management team has identified and rather than give up equity and thereby spread

the risk (and the upside if it works), they get greedy. The belief is that this money can be borrowed and deployed with returns that meet certain size and timing assumptions. When those assumptions turn out to be wrong and the profits are delayed or less than anticipated, the burden of that excessive optimism comes home to roost. Too much debt stresses cash and ultimately the viability of the business. Interest payments must be made. Debt must be repaid. Covenants must be met. When interest, repayments, and covenants are missed, management spends its time in workout meetings with the lender instead of running and growing the business. If severe enough, the existence of the business is threatened. Understanding the balance sheet and debt structure, interest rates, debt maturities, and robustness of lender relationships is crucial for all business owners and CFOs. Making sure there are adequate cash reserves to fund future debt obligations is mandatory.

To help me avoid excessive optimism, overleveraging, and the dreaded dumb tax, I have used a simple three-part formula for years. I am not saying it is perfect, but it has protected me from my tendency toward using my glands to run my businesses:

a. What is the upside?

b. What is the downside?

c. Can I live with the downside?

6. **⚿ Excess Capacity Risk:** Every business has under-utilized assets or excess production capability that can either be made more productive or eliminated from the business's cost or capital structure. Examples might include staff (C-level players are the worst), inventory, excessive receivables (or receivable days), production capability, knowledge, strategic relationships, expertise, office or warehouse space, alliances, etc. ⚿ A key component of running the business end of your business is correctly identifying where the business should allocate its resources. If resources are idle or lacking in productivity, a great business owner will strike immediately and remedy this waste.

The myth that entrepreneurs are risk-takers is misguided. The entrepreneurs you read about in *The Wall Street Journal* and *Forbes* magazine have taken *calculated* risks. They understood what could go wrong, had a "Plan B," and managed their business to minimize the probability and cost in the event of a mistake.

Ignoring the internal and external risks and how these risks could affect your business if they occur will prove to be a costly mistake.

Chapter 17

Conclusion:
All Skills Are Learnable

The vast majority of business owners around the world are struggling financially, and sadly, they will continue that way. They leak profits and cash flow and don't know where the leaks are or how to plug them. They guess when it comes to making their business and financial decisions. They feel like gerbils on a treadmill, running faster and faster, growing increasingly tired and frustrated, and never fully achieving their financial goals or potential. Ultimately they either work way harder than they need to, sabotage their business, or die of exhaustion.

The reason is simple. You cannot win the game of business without having the required business skills and optics. And without a scoreboard, you're doomed.

Here are two fundamental truths:

1. What got you here won't get you there. If it could get
    you there, you would already be there, and you're not,
    so it won't.

2. Good is not good enough. Warren Buffett observed
    that General Motors was a good company—and that
    was the problem. In today's world being a *good* com-
    pany is a prescription for mediocrity and disaster. If you
    want to succeed, you must be *outstanding*.

You did not start your business to make it small, play second
fiddle, or take a backseat. Lowering your expectations or staying frustrated by having a conversation in your head about how hard things
are is clearly not the answer. Making the commitment to find solutions and learn what you need to know is.

⚷ Albert Einstein nailed it when he said, "The true crisis is the
crisis of incompetence. The greatest fault with people is the laziness
with which they attempt to find solutions to their problems."

So regardless of your industry, size, or level of success, the critical
questions remain the same:

- How can I be smarter and more competitive?

- How can I add more value and make fewer mistakes?

- How can I rapidly find the leaks that are costing me
  profits and cash flow? How can I get them permanently
  plugged?

- How can I take the guesswork out of my decision making and take control of my business and finances?

- What are the critical drivers I must monitor to optimize and maximize my profits and cash flow?

- How can I be more efficient with my business prioritization and activities?

- How can I move the needle with the least amount of wasted motion?

Check out other ways you can learn from me by reading the next chapter on Growth Opportunities, calling us, or visiting www.KeystotheVault.com to find out more.

Chapter 18

Keys to the Vault®: *Growth Opportunities*

I have spent the past forty years of my business career:

1. Mastering the critical business drivers and levers.

2. Learning, practicing, and refining the distinctions and lessons that make the difference.

These drivers, levers, and distinctions serve as the foundation for all my teaching and writing and for the curriculum of the Keys to the Vault® Business School.

I have distilled the past forty years of successes and mistakes down to the key business strategies. The curriculum I have created and teach in the Keys to the Vault® Business School includes different programs, courses, and skills that are all designed to help you accelerate your business and financial performance and success.

- **4-Day MBA®:** A four-day classroom course in which I answer the most frequent question I receive when traveling around the world speaking and teaching on business: "Keith, how do I grow my business and make more money?" Regardless of where I speak, business owners tell me they feel like they have a job, not a business. They feel like their business is running them, when they should be running their business. In the 4-Day MBA®, you will learn the most critical skills and tools required to run the business end of your business, the skills to grow from "operator" to "owner," and how to convert your "job" into a business that has lasting value. A critical part of owner skills is financial literacy and mastering the fundamentals of financial statements, financial statement analysis, and business optics. At the end of the second day, I will hand out the financial statements of a disguised Fortune 100 company and, by looking only at the numbers, you will be able to decide if you do or don't want to own the stock. And you'll be right.

- **How to Buy (or Exit) a Business®:** A four-day classroom program that is exceptionally powerful. Many people would like to own a business but want to avoid the hard work, uncertainty, and risk associated with a start-up. Many existing business owners would like to expand via acquisition, as it is usually easier and less expensive to buy a customer than it is to win them over. Knowing how to find good companies for sale, how to locate and work with a broker, what specific questions to ask the seller and how to earn the seller's confidence, how to evaluate, how to perform the due diligence, how to value the business, how to raise the money, and how to structure the deal and calculate the purchase price are all included. Students receive a comprehensive how-to reference manual, in addition to working on real-life examples in the classroom. Creating a valuable business that you can exit is the flip side of buying a business. The four critical business strategies you learn at How to Buy (or Exit) a Business are:

1. Optimizing your exitability.

2. Maximizing your exit value.

3. Growth by acquisition.

4. Acquisition/selling skills and tool belt.

- **Plan or Get Slaughtered®**: A two-day classroom program that focuses exclusively on successfully driving revenue. Most business owners have had the experience of hitting an invisible ceiling on top-line growth. You have a goal of increasing revenue by 10 or 25 or 50 percent, but you don't have an actual plan to produce the desired growth. This course teaches the strategic and tactical growth strategies required to achieve this growth and gives you actual classroom time to do the critical thinking to create that plan.

- **Board of Directors**: As business owners, we tend to be astonishingly optimistic in our thinking and planning.

We rarely question our assumptions, nor do we have experienced business advisers watching our progress or providing us with feedback. As a result, we commit the most fatal of mistakes: running in the wrong direction enthusiastically. The Board of Directors is an exclusive (by invitation only) twelve-month program in which fifteen entrepreneurs and business owners—who are actually in business, have revenue, and are "doing it"—meet with me three to four times per year for two or three days per meeting. I serve as chairman of the Board. As a Board member, you have access to me for additional support, as needed, during the Board year. Having a Board of Directors who will advise, counsel, direct, set strategic direction, monitor execution and accountability, review monthly and quarterly financial statements, review your annual plan, and provide optics—both opportunities and icebergs—is critical if you expect to achieve the goals of your business and generate new strategies to build, grow, market, expand, and diversify your company.

- **Private One-on-One Consulting**: Business owners, management teams, and entrepreneurs who require private, personal advice and consulting can customize time with me. Private Consulting can range from half to full days, to monthly or quarterly sessions spread out over six to twelve months. Having access to a private adviser is an exceptionally powerful way to leverage your time and your results.

If you're done wasting time and money lurching from shiny pennies to magic bullets to fast-buck schemes, if you know there is a gap in your skills and tools, if you are committed to doing what it takes to achieve the results you desire and deserve, and if you are serious about reaching your full potential and breaking through as a business owner, I want to encourage you to:

🔑 *Invest in yourself,* which is the key to growth.

🔑 *Learn the critical distinctions so you can create better choices,* which is the key to a better life.

🔑 *Do whatever it takes to create excellence, mastery, and contribution,* which are the keys to fulfillment.

Please contact us either through email or our websites. If you're looking for answers, I can help.

info@KeystotheVault.com

www.KeystotheVault.com

www.CFOScoreboard.com

512-231-9944

Appendix A

Rolling 13-Week Cash Flow Forecast

A Rolling 13-Week Cash Flow Forecast consists of four parts:

1. A beginning cash balance (which will always be the ending cash balance from the week immediately prior).

2. *Projected* Sources and Receipts of cash (which would include cash sales; collections on receivables; the cash proceeds on the sale of property, plant, or equipment; money raised from banks or lenders, etc.). In essence, this would include any cash that would be deposited into your bank account.

3. *Projected* Uses, Payments, and Expenditures of cash (which would include all bills paid, purchases of inventory, deposits paid, loans repaid, or accounts payable paid, etc.). In essence, this would include any cash that would be spent or disbursed out of your bank account.

4. An ending cash balance (which is simply the sum of 1–3 above).

Your spreadsheet will have 14 columns, one for each of the next

13 weeks and one to use "after-the-fact" to compare your *actual* results in week one with the *projected* results for week one. This weekly after-the-fact comparison is critical because it allows you to accurately modify and update your projections for the next week based on actual results from the week that just ended.

After the basic template is set up, here is the process we use:

1. Make a thorough list of all the sources and uses of cash. Lots of detail leads to better optics, or said another way: 🔑 Generalizations kill clarity. So, for example, do not show just one line for "accounts receivable." Instead, make a list of the customers who owe you money and estimate the amount you think they will pay in the appropriate week's column. You usually have much greater control over the timing of when you will pay your bills than when you will collect your money, but some payments, like payroll, rent, and note payments are not only recurring but also mandatory. Other payments might have latitude on the timing; you can make use of this flexibility to craft a cash flow forecast based on your anticipated cash sources.

2. Obviously, the farther out you forecast, the less precise your projections will be. The first couple of weeks will be much more accurate than weeks twelve or thirteen, but that doesn't mean you shouldn't be estimating timing and amounts. Do not let perfect get in the way of possible on this exercise. A good guess is better than ignorance.

3. After the thirteen weeks have been estimated and recorded into your forecast, the next update will be at the conclusion of week one. Your spreadsheet will have a column for week one's actual results and you will record week one's actual sources and uses of cash in this column. You might have estimated you would collect $1,600 from Mr. Gotcha but only collected $1,000. Record $1,000 in the actual column. You might not have estimated paying any money to Ms. Ransom, but she called and demanded payment so you coughed up $2,300. Record $2,300 in the actual column. Based on your actual results in week one, you will do five things:

   a. Update your ending cash balance for the end of week one with the actual cash balance (which is about to be the new week one).

   b. Update and refine all of the sources and uses line items for the next twelve weeks based on your actual historical results from week one.

   c. Roll all your weeks forward one week. The old week two will become the new week one. The old week three will become the new week two and so forth.

   d. Add a new column for the new thirteenth week and fill in (as best you can) all the anticipated sources and uses for that week.

   e. Update your projected weekly ending cash balances based on (a), (b), and (c) above.

Some business owners do better using a two-week cycle rather than one week. This is good, too. Candidly, using a thirty-day cycle is better than doing zero cash flow forecasting.

Keep in mind this is a living analysis, and therefore will always be changing. Stuff will happen that you didn't anticipate (both timing and amounts), which will necessitate updates and modifications to your plan. If you see a wall looming on the horizon that has no easy solution, the Rolling 13-Week Cash Flow Forecast will serve as an early warning system so you can make adjustments. For example, if you notice cash getting thin (or negative) in week five, you might need to think about calling Mr. Gotcha in week four or letting Ms. Ransom know she will not get paid until week six. In other words, you should shift around the timing of your cash receipts or uses based on the results you anticipate occurring and take action accordingly. It does no good to know you will run out of cash in week ten and then do nothing about it in weeks one through nine. Use the Rolling 13-Week Cash Flow Forecast not only as a planning tool but also as an action plan to ensure the oxygen keeps flowing into your business.

Big-picture cash shortfalls can be dealt with in a limited number of ways:

1. Collect more cash revenue or deposits (generates operating cash).

2. Accelerate the timing of accounts receivable collections, which reduces receivable days (generates operating cash).

3. Reduce expenses (increases operating cash).

4. Delay payments on accounts payable, which increases payable days (increases operating cash).

5. Spend less on inventory purchases (increases operating cash).

6. Delay buying, or purchase fewer or cheaper property, plant, and equipment assets (reduces investing cash needs).

7. Sell some property plant and equipment (generates investing cash).

8. Borrow money from the bank (generates financing cash).

9. Raise money from investors (generates financing cash).

Keep in mind that none of these nine possible solutions will be implemented unless you have the optics to know there is a problem. The following Excel chart is a simple example of the first five weeks of a Rolling 13-Week Cash Flow Forecast.

KEYS TO THE VAULT.

Today's Date is:
Business Name: Toadies

Rolling Weekly Cash Flow Forecast

Cash Flow Forecast	Actual Cash Flow Results	Forecast for Time Period	Forecast for Time Period	Forecast for Time Period	Forecast for Time Period	Forecast for Time Period
	Current Week-Actual	8/10/2014 to 8/16/2014	8/17/2014 to 8/23/2014	8/24/2014 to 8/30/2014	8/31/2014 to 9/6/2014	9/7/2014 to 9/13/2014
13 Week Forecast		1	2	3	4	5
Beginning Cash	110,501	25,045	3,045	(955)	(1,955)	(8,455)

Cash Sources and Receipts — Enter category names below.

Product Sells	150,000	150,000	150,000	175,000	175,000	175,000
Installation	90,000	90,000	90,000	95,000	90,000	90,000
Service	45,000	45,000	45,000	90,000	45,000	45,000
Receivables	3,500	3,500	40,000	15,000	10,000	9,000
ABC	1,500	2,000	0	0	0	6,000
Mr Gotcha	2,000	1,500	0	0	2,500	0
BeMore Construction	0	0	5,000	0	2,500	0
Total Cash Available	288,500	292,000	330,000	375,000	325,000	325,000

Cash Uses, Payments or Expenditures — Enter category names below.

Advertising	5,500	5,500	5,500	10,000	5,500	5,500
Services	25,000	25,000	25,000	25,000	25,000	25,000
Parking/Building/Lease	50,000	50,000	50,000	50,000	50,000	50,000
Inventory	80,000	75,000	80,000	50,000	50,000	100,000
Vehicle	5,000	5,000	5,000	7,500	7,500	7,500
Equipment	5,000	5,000	5,000	5,000	25,000	4,000
Payroll	150,000	125,000	125,000	150,000	125,000	150,000
Property Tax	0	0	0	15,000	0	0
Supplies	10,500	10,500	10,500	10,500	10,500	10,500
Utilities	13,000	13,000	13,000	13,000	13,000	13,000
Below the Line Items	40,000	0	15,000	40,000	20,000	40,000
Total Cash Usage	384,000	314,000	334,000	376,000	331,500	405,500

Ending Cash	15,001	3,045	(955)	(1,955)	(8,455)	(88,955)

About the Author

Keith J. Cunningham is a seasoned entrepreneur, business owner, international speaker, and acclaimed author. He is regarded as one of the world's foremost authorities on business mastery. With more than forty years of business and investing experience, Keith has taught critical business skills to thousands of management teams and business owners around the world. Keith teaches the tools and strategies used by the pros not only to make more money, but more importantly, to keep it, grow it, and maximize it.

Keith is an expert at helping business owners turn their businesses into highly profitable companies with explosive growth. In Keith's Keys to the Vault® Business School, he teaches the detailed strategies you can implement even in today's uncertain economy to ensure your revenues, profits, and cash flow soar.

That's *The Ultimate Blueprint for an Insanely Successful Business.*

Index